DATE DUE

APR 16 98			

DEMCO 38-296

ON SECOND THOUGHT

A COMPILATION

AMERICAN INDIAN LITERATURE AND CRITICAL STUDIES SERIES
Gerald Vizenor and Louis Owens, General Editors

ALSO BY MAURICE KENNY

Poetry
Blackrobe: Isaac Jogues
Between Two Rivers: Selected Poems
Greyhounding This America
Last Mornings in Brooklyn
Tekonwatonti: Molly Brant, Poems of War, 1735–1795

Fiction
Rain and Other Fictions

On Second Thought

A COMPILATION

BY MAURICE KENNY

WITH A FOREWORD BY
JOSEPH BRUCHAC / GREEN CORN MOON

UNIVERSITY OF OKLAHOMA PRESS : NORMAN AND LONDON

...us assistance of Edith Gaylord Harper.

...ception of brief quotations within the
...eproduced in any form without prior
written permission from the publisher.

Fictional names, characters, places, and incidents are the products of the author's imagination, and any resemblance to actual events, locales, or persons, living or dead, is entirely coincidental.

Library of Congress Cataloging-in-Publication Data
Kenny, Maurice, 1929-
    On second thought : a compilation / by Maurice Kenny ; with a foreword by Joseph Bruchac/Green Corn Moon.
        p.   cm. —(American Indian literature and critical studies series ; v. 18)
        ISBN 0-8061-2766-X (alk. paper)
        1. Mohawk Indians—Literary collections.   2. Kenny, Maurice, 1929-
—Biography.   3. Authors,   American—20th   century—Biography.
4. Mohawk   Indians—Biography.   I. Bruchac,   Joseph,   1942- .
II. Title.   III. Series.
PS3561.E4905 1995
811'.54—dc20   95-5891
                                                                      CIP

Book design by Cathy Carney Imboden.

The paper in this book meets the guidelines for permanence and durability of the Committee on Production Guidelines for Book Longevity of the Council on Library Resources, Inc. ⊗

On Second Thought: A Compilation is Volume 18 in the American Indian Literature and Critical Studies Series.

1   2   3   4   5   6   7   8   9   10

For
      Werner Beyer
      Douglas Angus
      Rochelle and George
      Martha Millard, my niece
And especially
      in memory of my father
      Andrew Kenny
      and my friends
      Diane Decorah
      Lorne Simon
      who remain beautiful in the spirit world

CONTENTS

THE POETIC CAREER OF MAURICE KENNY

It would be difficult to imagine the shape of contemporary Native American writing without the presence of Maurice Kenny. Although his autobiographical essay is characteristically modest in its understatement of his place as a poetic mentor and innovator, I cannot think of another American Indian poet who has affected as many lives for as long a time and in as many positive ways.

It is, almost, as if there are many Maurice Kennys. There is the Maurice Kenny who is a prolific poet and one of the earliest Native poetic voices to be heard in the second half of this century—well before the emergence of even N. Scott Momaday and Simon Ortiz. A master lyricist, Kenny is also the creator of a new form of dramatic monologue in his book-length recreations of the voices and times of Isaac Jogues, the misled Jesuit priest among the Iroquois, and Molly Brant, the fiery Mohawk woman whose intelligence and passion affected the course of American history in the mid-1700s.

There is also the Maurice Kenny who is one of the finest readers of his own poetry of this century, a man who outdoes most of the new "performance poets" with his dramatic flair and in the rolling cadence of his voice. I cannot tell you how many times I have seen Maurice quietly ascend the stage—in the eyes of those in the audience who had never seen him before, nothing more than a small, slightly frail-looking man with his hair in a grey ponytail—peer out at the people with that eagle's look in his eye, take a breath and then with his first words, transform himself into a presence as powerful and memorable as that of Heno, the Iroquois god of thunder, his phrases as sharp as flint, as sweet as wild strawberries.

There is also the Maurice Kenny who, as editor of *Contact/II* and Strawberry Press, has played a seminal role in the careers of a generation of young American writers. Although his work may be most evident in his support of contemporary Native writing and his tireless labors to bring it more strongly into the body of world literature where it belongs, his career as an editor has always been devoted to multiculturalism in the truest and most intelligent sense of that concept of literary diversity—a concept which he lived before it became the often misunderstood buzz word of the 1990s. That he did this on the smallest of budgets and without the backing of either a major press or a university—the kind of backing which other major figures in the literary movements of this second half of our century often seem to enjoy—is a tribute to his indefatigable energy and ingenuity. Once again an image comes to my mind, the image of Maurice Kenny wrestling boxes of his own books and the books he published by other writers onto the subway to carry them to a poetry reading or a book fair. I see him pause, put down the carton and lean back, his hand to his chest as his heart complains. Then he takes a deep breath, picks that heavy box up again and continues onward.

Then there is the Maurice Kenny who has been a teacher, a career which he came to late in life after his return from decades in Brooklyn (where he had been mugged on the stairs of his own apartment building) to the homeland of his Mohawk father in northern New York state. The lessons he learned as a young poet bruised by the thoughtless words of mentors he trusted are lessons that have shaped his style as an instructor. Tough intelligence and intuitive empathy are rarely combined in a teacher, but those elements resulted in his being one of the best-loved faculty members of every college fortunate enough to have him on its staff—whether North Country Community College in Saranac Lake, New

York, or the University of Oklahoma, or the En'owkin Centre in British Columbia.

Tough intelligence and intuitive empathy are good descriptions of every part of Maurice Kenny's public career. And if we add in that love of language which characterizes all of his writing, a love every great poet must cherish, we are close to a partial understanding of the place Maurice Kenny holds today in literature, a place which should outlast the trends and fads of this century. In 1992 a gathering of writers took place in Oklahoma, a festival which brought together more than three hundred American Indian writers from throughout the hemisphere. Not surprisingly, Maurice Kenny was one of the major forces behind that gathering and wore himself out for its four days coordinating more than a dozen readings by the various poets and fiction writers. The name of that once-in-a-lifetime festival now comes to my mind as I consider the career of Maurice Kenny, for it was called "Returning the Gift." As poet, performer, editor, and teacher, Maurice has spent four decades doing just that, giving, continuing to give, and returning thanks for all that he has been given.

Joseph Bruchac/Green Corn Moon

August 1994

No creative work is created by wishing it so. Images, objects, and ideas result from the supermarket of a life, parents, playmates, teachers, friends, editors, and most assuredly, one's culture and tradition. My poems and stories have been given to me from all of the above. I've listened and borrowed, translated, rendered, changed. A story, "Wet Moccasins," was lifted directly from my friend Peg Roy. Some years back, as a guest poet at the MLA Washington, D.C., conference, I had the pleasure of meeting Margaret Atwood. Over breakfast, I confessed I could not read her poetry. Obviously, she was startled, confronted with such a statement. I explained the reason was that I enjoyed her poems so very much that occasionally I lifted objects, style, and sometimes images or a whole line. She smiled and offered her confession. "Don't worry," she said. "I've been stealing all my life." And we do—all our lives, with the hope writers who come after us will steal from our work. It is called tradition, the tradition and culture of one's life, of literature itself—tribal, American, and European classic. I have borrowed from Leslie Silko as much as I have borrowed from Walt Whitman and Robinson Jeffers. I have borrowed much from Native lore, Iroquois legend, American history—which does certainly include tribal, modern, and contemporary Native American culture, which is beautiful and meaningful however tragic (yet resilient) it has been since contact with the European. I have even been known, though unobtrusively, to borrow from students—at least, if nothing more, an idea or catchy contemporary phrase. I believe the teacher can learn from the student, from the young as well as the wizened of wisdom. I have learned and listened to the voices of the real—the hawk and the wind in chicory, the river—and the voices that come from that distant and ancient past, the voices of the ancestors. Some might call this the atavistic theory of Carl Jung.

There are people deserving of thanks in regard to this collection, such editors as Madge and Murray Heller, Dan Littlefield, Anna Lee Walters, Robin Kay Willoughby, Larry Jackson, Frank Parman, and particularly Elaine and Dennis Maloney of White Pine Press, who continue to support my creativity and have gifted me with handsome books created out of their own beauty and vision.

I need to thank graciously my various interns, work-studies, and typists: Daniel Bodah, Brett Sanchi—as well as Todd Wilson, Chad Sweeney, Laura Mahon, and Matt McGowan. I wish also to thank Tim Jock, Kathleen Leone, Ruth Woodward, and Dean Roczen, who have offered so very much support. And because I love them dearly, and because they are beautiful and sensitive, and excellent drivers, I also wish to thank deeply, sincerely, my good friends and former students Thuy and Nick, Lori, Deborah, Shane, Jamie, and Lorne. A word of gratitude must be extended also to Jim Ruppert, Michael Castro, Gerald Vizenor, A. LaVonne Brown Ruoff, Geary Hobson, Alan Velie, R. M. Davis, Louis Cook, and Ellen Rocco of WSLU-FM, Nathan Farb, who has been an important inspiration, and my astute editor, Sarah Morrison.

It behooves me to thank the various administrators of Poets and Writers, Inc., whose funding has certainly helped pay the rent these many years; and also Rachel Guido-DeVries, Director of the Community Writers Project in Syracuse, N.Y., who "fed me summer" after I received a fellowship and residence from the New York State Council of the Arts for 1992. Lastly, I thank Jeanette Armstrong and Don Fiddler of the En'owkin Centre (a unit of the University of Victoria) in Penticton, B.C., for their warmth, understanding, generosity, and employment during the 1991–92 academic term.

Of course I will not forget the folks who cooked me suppers and gave pillows to the head over all these years: Wanda and Julian, Wendy and Arthur, the late Donna Smith and Mary Dickson, Larry and Paul, Ruth and David, Ken and Sue, Georgina and Nick, John and Eva, Peg, Jolene, Ray Fadden, and Peter Jemison, with whom I worked four years when I was poet-in-residence at the American Indian Community House in N.Y.C.

This is what I mean by tradition, culture, and tribe. They have loaned to my borrowing, which I now return with heartfelt appreciation.

Oneh. Niaweh.

Maurice Kenny

PART ONE

INTRODUCTION

A MEMOIR

1 January. Windy British Columbia. I have just returned from Oklahoma, where a few slivers of sun spoked the plains. In Penticton, Canada, the Monashee range of the eastern Cascade slopes rises from Lake Skaha's slate-gray waters, white caps swirling across liquid depths. Coyote winds howl across this Okanagan valley, which is usually burning hot, semiarid, a valley springtimed with blossoming apple and peach, cherry and pear and walnut. Now the mountains' stripped, craggy fingers reach into an overcast sky. It is a continuous eastern November. The constant winter moisture penetrates the flesh; the whole sky shakes, shivers from this unrelenting force, the weather.

At home, six inches of snow cover the ground and the frozen lakes. Probably it is twenty to thirty degrees below zero. The bears are caved. Men carve huge ice blocks out of the lake for winter carnival. The palace will rise in flood-light colors of blue and pale berry, lime and lemon. The organizers are working on floats for the grand parade. A chili cook-off was just won. Tamaracks pierce the blue sky, naked, shorn of needles—the only conifer that sheds.

The house on the hill overlooking the village of Saranac Lake is empty. No Sula—my twelve-year-old cat, yellow and white, terrified of violence—kills for a cookie or a plate of sour cream. No plants. The African violets farmed out with Sula to friends, Ruth and Brett. No one sitting at the round kitchen table. No Scrabble; no Peg winning and bragging about her high score. No students stalking the refrigerator. No Dean blasting his tunes on the stereo. I'm numb. Teeth crunch down on Christmas shortbread John and Jeanne sent from their woodsy kitchen. I taste home, smell the wood stove, the chopped-pine scent rising into the air. I smell the fresh cedar by the backdoor, stew bubbling on the burner, corn bread baking in the oven. Empty. The house is empty. Only the books and curios tell that human beings once inhabited this home. Sun slants through the forest cathedral across the road. One crow caws through the trees white with winter blossoms of snow. Sun, which would warm the now-aging bones, take away the chill of northwest Canada. Help to alleviate the grumbles of arthritis that grip the right leg, its bones never bitten before by this gnawing pain.

What am I doing here in this cold mountain country? Why am I so heartsick for home, the empty house on the hill, the touch of Sula's fur, Dean's rock and roll music, the African violet's rich purple blossoms (a plant my mother could never grow successfully), the kitchen and the table, and the crowd of voices lifting forks of roast chicken or tuna casserole, or plain old spaghetti? What am I doing so far away from home? There are the graves of my father and mother, my blood, the earth where my own dust will settle, the red-tailed hawk of Ray Fadden, and his bears. Why do I walk in this valley of the Cascades and not the Adirondacks, the home of the Mohawk and the Algonquin those long centuries ago? On the sacred mountain youths went to prepare and experience the first vision, the quest through dreams brought by prayer and fasting from food and water. Surely there is a sacred mountain here in the Monashee range, in the Cascades. Here in the country of the Okanagan people their reserve must have many holy places.

Every place of beauty is holy in this land, sacred. Every mountain peak, each river that flows down to the sea, each handful of earth in the palm, each wolf howl, bear growl, thrush song, child cry. But I am a stranger among strangers, an alien spirit amongst these apple orchards, the pear and cherry. This lonely foot hikes the Skaha shore and beach, looking up to the Monashee and trying to find home in these mountains, a sacred place to take myself, to forget myself, to become part of this rich and beautiful place, the Okanagan. Cold though it now is, and windy and damp.

I came to this new land, this country to teach.

2 Growing up is very hard to do. Growing up Indian in the United States is very hard to do. Growing up a half-blood is painful. Growing up a writer/poet is almost impossible. Filling in the blanks between these various aspects of life

may prove to be even more difficult: first, locating the puzzle, then the pieces, and discovering the blank spots for the pieces to fit into the jigsaw. The whens, whys, and wherefores. Plus the possible embarrassments to you and yours. Going from A to what ever alphabet letter you stop on can cause pain and anger to rise up from not only your own being but the downright hostile motives of those who become adjuncts to you, the subject. Where do you begin, end? What do you reveal, eliminate, emphasize, discreetly lighten up on? I believe it was Jean Jacques Rousseau who said that the writer always must seek for truth, and I agree, but is this possible in the composition of an autobiographical piece? Should the truth be abandoned for sincerity? Truth may have nothing whatsoever to do with the vividness of memory, its sparkle or dulled edge.

Years do dull the edge. Nothing remains rapier sharp. Who remembers what he had for breakfast yesterday, the tie worn Monday, why you played the ace of spades when you knew who had the queen of spades in the game of hearts? Can memory be trusted to be utterly truthful? Is truth equal with fact? The scientist deals with facts, the poet with beauty, and is there truth in beauty? (Ignore John Keats for the moment.) Beauty is in the eye of the beholder. If that is true, then is truth in the eye of the sayer who is a beholder as well? And is the truth of the Mohawk the same as the truth of the Hopi?

All tribal mores deal with the concept of truth. It was wrong to lie to your own people, chief, village, but it was near heroic to lie to the white invader of your homeland. And what is the truth of Christianity? (We know its beauty.) There are more sects nearly each day. Should we live by the Bible, the sword, the word of Jesus Christ, Jung's collective oversoul, or the echoes of time itself? Perhaps we merely count the rings of a virgin pine and claim these rings to be the absolute, the truth of humanity and all life around us. But, what of the tree's memory? Does it fade after the first one hundred years? Can it be factual? So much depends on "a red wheelbarrow." Famines may have passed this pine, insects, snows, or lack of snows. Can the circles be trusted? The tree too has a memory that may fill it from season to season. I would as soon trust last night's dream or nightmare. It rises from the soul, the being, the essence, the fears and joys, the subconscious, through a motif of symbolic images — "a red wheelbarrow." William Carlos Williams was right: "This is just to say / I ate the plums. . . ."

And that is what I have done. I have eaten the plums "so cold and so sweet." I remember most things, and yes, I do remember what I had for breakfast yesterday (a toasted roll with blackberry jam and the ever-present mug of black coffee). Memory is fairly sound; beauty is wished for; truth is of the utmost in this presentation, but only as far as memory allows. The art of dodging, I can master that sport.

3   *Telemachus: A Précis*

Had I listened all those years ago to the evaluations of my work by John Crowe Ransom, I would never have shelved twenty-four collections of poetry and fiction. Ransom, obviously a fine but minor American poet, had an ear for European classical forms and a restricted rhythm. My successful rhythms do not hark back to Milton and Donne, or even Longfellow. These many years later, I find it hard to believe that Ransom would allow even Whitman a place in his canon, and possibly not Robinson Jeffers either. Certainly he would ignore the rhythms of the contemporary poets Baraka, Ginsberg, Rothenberg, and yes, even Diane Wakowski, Susan Howe, or the late Audre Lorde.

While at Butler University in the early 1950s, I wrote out my mix-metaphored heart into poems. Perhaps I was wild, or eccentric (if a youth can be so), but I abandoned my whole being to poetry, believing that I grasped some modicum of magic in my language. And I did attempt occasionally to write in classical forms, but to my eye and ear these poems were utter failures. When working in free verse — without knowing at the time that it was free verse and as such a recognized form to a few—I felt I had an accomplishment in my poems because the language, the images, and especially, the rhythms came naturally, perhaps even atavistically—like "leaves to a bough," as Keats had suggested. I did admire the classic poets, and Donne was a favorite of mine as a young student, as were Blake and Keats, and the Greeks in translation. Candidly, however, I have to say my poetic reflections of their achievements were failures. Actually, they were more like imitations, especially of Wordsworth.

I was fortunate to have differing instructors for different poetry courses. I took every literature and writing course offered—even advanced composition, although my spelling and syntax presented great problems. My syntax was nurtured to some degree to health by a Dr. Graham, but my spelling has remained inconsistent and doubtful to a shameful degree.

I signed up for a course in modern poetry taught by the poet Roy Marz—a good man, an intelligent mind, and a lecturer of critical astuteness. He brought my attention to Gerard Manley Hopkins, Edward Arlington Robinson, and Robinson Jeffers. Dr. Marz paid scant attention to Sandburg, Kenneth Fearing, and William Carlos Williams, and the only women he taught were Amy Lowell and Gertrude Stein, neither of whom he greatly admired. He favored the more religious or divine—not necessarily mystical—poets, especially Hopkins and, to a large extent, Eliot. That was fine with me. At the time I was having a bout with spirituality and particularly with my own spirit and faith. Wordsworth's pantheism was appealing and was very credible to my widening mind.

I guess one might say Roy Marz was a classicist. His own devotional poems were often written in sonnet form. We young writer-students hunted out his published poems in various magazines, especially in *Poetry*, where he was published often. I knew instantly upon reading Roy's poems that he would see little worth in my juvenile work. And it came to pass that he found small merit in my poems, and did not bite the lip or spare the red pen in his critical remarks. I was lucky to print a poem or two in the English department's literary magazine, *Mss.*, which also published several essays I had written for Dr. Graham's composition course. Roy read both, naturally; I believe he was faculty advisor to the journal. I managed to persuade the jury of student editors to print a poem concerning the life and death, in 1953, of Dylan Thomas, the most magical lyric poet of his day. Thomas was a poet I found it easy to take to—or was it his rather sodden poverty and drunken lifestyle? Most students are poor, and most enjoy a cheap bottle of Chianti when extra coins jingle in their pockets.

I have never allowed the Thomas poem to be reprinted, it being sheer juvenalia—nor other silly poems I was publishing at that time in the Indianapolis newspapers. These poems were written in a style that today would appear to be influenced by Charles Olson's projective verse, but honestly, in the early fifties I had never heard of Olson and his Black Mountain school of poetry.

Although Roy Marz was probably correct in his evaluations of the poems I was composing as a student at Butler University, I felt then, and know now, my burning need to write, to express my feelings, to record events and ideas, and to sing. I did not sing well, but surely he must have seen some raw (perhaps bloody) talent. He mildly praised the essays published in *Mss.*, and he praised a novel I was then writing for Werner Beyer's Creative Writing and Writers' Workshop.

Werner Beyer was my real mentor. I practically forced this generous instructor, a Keats and Coleridge scholar, to become my big brother or second father—a habit I've never broken with the many males who have come into my life. Being the only boy among three children certainly caused me to hunger for a brother, and being a thousand miles away from my father in Watertown, New York, caused me to develop a dire need for a father figure—one who could understand and support a young writer.

I wrote few poems for Dr. Beyer. I was somewhat terrified of his rarified position as the author of *Keats and the Daemon King*. A brilliant man—as was Roy Marz—Beyer dealt with the truly classic while Marz taught modern and contemporary literature. I took numerous classes under Beyer's tutelage: a survey of world literature (a full-year course), Romantic poetry and prose, two writing courses, etc. He challenged every period I ever dropped onto a sheet of paper, whether in a creative composition, a classroom exercise, or a term paper. I hoed the row, and it proved beneficial. Beyer did offer rewards—spaghetti suppers at his home, which his young wife, Ruth, prepared for his Writers' Workshop students (all four of us— he only allowed four in the class) and tickets to the Indianapolis Symphony—which I couldn't possibly afford from my meager wages as a sundry clerk in Haag's Drugstore. More important than the above, he offered strong support, badly needed praise, and good sense, as well as strong critiques of all I wrote. I deeply desired to please him and worked extra hard to move the first C up to an A in his classes, but more to the point, I wanted to receive his commendation on my creative output, the stories and the novella I was working on. He suggested I send the novella to Houghton Mifflin in Boston, which offered an annual prize and publication of the best original manuscript submitted during the year. I turned to stone—a cold-footed coward. Neither did I send the manuscript, nor did I finish the novella.

Odd, but years later I met in New York City one of the winners of that $10,000 prize, Edward Hoagland, who has gone on to great success and honors as both novelist and journalist. We lived in the same building in New York, lofts on the corner of Bleeker and Lafayette. Well, I lived there, and Ed lived elsewhere with his then wife, but rented a studio in the same block building. I was impressed with his writing skills and notoriety. He'd been reviewed in the *New York Times*. I, too, was by that time published. The *Watertown Daily Times* had privately printed *The Hopeless Kill*, and a new Beat press, Troubador, had published *Dead Letters Sent*. Troubador was to be the competition and East Coast counterpart to City Lights

Books in San Francisco. I gave Ed a copy of *Dead Letters Sent*, and he had some pleasant words to offer on several of the poems. He spoke with a bad stutter—though he was teaching at the New School—and his stutter confused my understanding of his critiques. We had some healthy chats on various subjects, especially animals. He had worked in a circus when very young, with the travelling, caged animals, especially the cats. I enjoyed his apparent confidence, which his stutter did not belie. Once he left the building I never saw him again. People have that way—they come and go, shutting doors behind them. Oh my, the friends and acquaintances I've lost through this method or style—to my regret now.

I've digressed away from John Crowe Ransom and Roy Marz. I timidly complained to friends concerning Dr. Marz's sharp criticism of my poems. One close buddy in particular, the late Robert Petty, advised I ship my poems out to a recognized author of repute. I chose Ransom, probably because he was then editor of the prestigious *Kenyon Review*. I trusted Bob Petty implicitly. He not only was a very fine poet, and a student editor of *Mss.*, but seemed to win all the poetry prizes at Butler University—which pricked my literary sensibilities but did not interfere with our friendship. Bob, a botany major, had had serious abdominal problems which bedded him in hospital for a lengthy period. We were close; took many hikes together; shared pleasures of high grades, contact with our various instructors on campus; and occasionally offered the succor of strong shoulders when things did not go well. I took Bob's advice and sent a batch of poems to Ransom. I don't recall a worse defeat.

Ransom emptied my spirit. He flagellated me with a dozen or less scalding words—"you have no sense of rhythm," etc. If a heart can break, then mine was shattered. In our huddles in the student union—which was really a routine cafeteria—my fellow student poets had shown some favorable response to my work. This group included Jack, who was an Eliot snob, and two grad students—all lit majors. Werner Beyer gave solid approval on my writing, as did Dr. Graham (he humorously named me "Young Charlie Lamb"), and in an oddly comforting way Roy Marz simply but firmly suggested I stick with prose. I was positive I was the new, perhaps reborn, Walt Whitman, in the America of the 1950s. Surely Whitman possessed pronounced rhythms. Had Ransom never read out loud "When Lilacs Last in the Dooryard Bloom'd," or "Out of the Cradle Endlessly Rocking," or even "Captain, My Captain"? Had he never enjoyed the symphonics of Poe, Hopkins, Dylan Thomas—all of whose music, rhythms, I savored, relished, and wished to imitate. How could this renowned man–editor–poet be so cruel, so heartless, as to destroy the rearing, vibrant spirit of a young poet? Surely Rilke would never have been so brutal, nor would William Carlos Williams with a single phrase wreak such havoc within the imagination and soul of a burgeoning poet.

I'm most grateful to Bob Petty, to the Eliot snob, to Werner Beyer, and to Douglas Angus, Louise Bogan, and Donald Allen for saving a drifting spirit from the fathomless depths of depression and numerous attempts at suicide.

As a writer, an editor, and an instructor of creative writing, I can look through poems and stories, I can scan a classroom today, and touch with my sight the endangered, desperate poet and fully realize the pain and disappointment waiting for their first turn in the literary world. The first rejection note may collapse their sense of security, which most likely took years to build—perhaps against all odds, including family, friends, and teachers not merely frowning but shaking the head, advising pursuit of the law or business, criminal justice, or pumping gasoline. I have an all-embracing empathy for the novice poet who sits on the limb of an oak tree while terrible monsters saw at the limb. True, not everyone is a writer. It is not true that there is a book in each and every one of us. The sensibility enters at birth and is directed over childhood by the many life forces around us—culminating in the sheer love of writing, a total fascination, a volcanic eruption of images and ideas. Poets are not born, they are made. To paraphrase Percy Shelley, "Life hurts you into poetry." Even

Roy Marz spoke of this: the creative person has suffered the slings and arrows of misfortune; the artist must suffer. Well, believe you me, I jumped onto the wagon early and fast. I would walk down the streets of Indianapolis hoping passersby would recognize the pain chiselled into my face. I supposed my countenance to be sober and somber, mute and mysterious, its brow and cheek creased from the misfortunes of life. My eyes downcast, my shoulders bent, I walked with an amble as if my legs could not carry the burden further. I was twenty-two.

After bidding adieus to Bob and Werner Beyer—who had, incidentally, confessed he had taught me all he had to teach and that now, perhaps, I should enter Northwestern University in Chicago, or maybe even Columbia, where he had studied under Mark Van Doren—I went home to my apartment, which I shared with another student-poet, drank as much wine as I could afford to buy, and downed as many as I could of the various pills that stood so invitingly on the medicine-chest shelf. My defeat was complete. Misunderstanding Dr. Beyer and listening more to Marz and Ransom, I walked for the first, though not the last, time into the realm of confused reaction. I was completely disempowered, to use a trendy and hackneyed word.

I remember sirens. I remember tubes forced into my mouth. I remember a policeman or hospital guard standing over me as I was strapped to a cot on wheels, and his voice echoing over and over—"You don't have to go to the bathroom; shut up." And then I felt his flashlight strike my bloated belly. I heard a scream.

What I remember next is sitting up in a bed within the confines of a large dim ward. An African-American man sat beside me. He uttered not a single word, but the warmth, concern, and kindness kindled in his eyes spoke of safety. Terror gripped. Where was I? I shrivelled in fear. Not of the youth sitting at my bedside combing my hair over and over again, but fear of the abstract, the unknown, the unremembered. Startled, I attempted to rise, but the young man very gently held me down, my head against the pillow. He continued to comb my hair. I fell asleep. When I woke next, another young man, in white, was seated beside me on the bed. The black man had disappeared into the dim shadows of the huge ward. It was night. It always seemed night; the few days—though it may have been weeks, it may have been months—were always dim and I was conscious of little but shadows. This man in white was the inquisitor. I cannot remember his questions nor my answers. He told me I was temporarily registered in the mental ward of an Indianapolis hospital and that he was there to help me. I remember peppery tears moving down my cheeks. He spoke fairly softly but adamantly, and the words he pronounced were firm. Yet all I recall—even a few months later, all I recalled—is that a voice called "Bob," and another called "Werner," had phoned.

There is no recollection of time, only dimness and shadows. Human zombies paced the ward, with cigarettes dangling from their lips or conducting the air with their fingers. The young black man rarely left my side and never ceased combing my hair. If I went to the bathroom he followed. If I was called from the ward, he followed to the locked door. If a nurse, or guard, or physician came to my bed, he was always there, the comb in his right hand, the smile of safety and security always on his brown lips, muscles flexed as weapons should I need his strength, his defense.

I never knew his name. I never asked, and he never offered to speak, to tell me.

Early one evening—I think it was evening—I woke from a medically induced nap to find the black man rigid at the foot of the bed, guarding. Another man in white stood near my head, which was down on the pillow. My brother-in-law stood beside him. He appeared worried. Tears were in his eyes. When I recognized Pat, I fell into sobs. The man in white asked, Did I know this stranger? Naturally, I did, but was amazed how he knew I was incarcerated in that ward. Pat revealed that my father had sent him to Indiana to bring me home. What relief! I stopped crying. He bent down and hugged me—though men do not hug, nor cry, nor feel. He lifted me off the bed. My street clothes were at the bottom of the bed, and Pat aided me in dressing.

At the door of the ward I turned to say goodbye to my black friend and companion. He was there. The comb was now in his shirt pocket. I think it was red. I can't now describe the emotion in his eyes and on his lips—but it seems that a door had closed on his life and the world had stopped. I looked as deeply as possible into the black pools of his eyes and thanked him with all my heart. He had probably saved my sanity. I could not give him a single word or sound of gratitude. I reached out my hand to touch his shoulder, but he wrenched back. As Pat and I hurriedly reeled through the doorway, I heard my comrade say, "Thank you. Goodbye."

Outside I found my sister Mary waiting with a container of medicine held tightly in her grasp. She was pale and as frightened as I was.

"A Dr. Beyer called Daddy," is all she said. All the way home to my father's house in Watertown, New York, that was the only expression Mary uttered. "Dr. Beyer called Daddy."

It was a quiet trip across an ominously black night.

There is, of course, no way I would ever dream of accusing John Crowe Ransom, or Roy, or Werner for my breakdown, which was without a doubt caused by strenuous work—study, reading until the tiny hours of the morning, stress at work at the drugstore, stress with finances, and general tension that invades the essence of us all. However, I have carefully kept and protected those brief conjectures of Ransom. They are in the same stout folder, behind stiff plastic, next to more positive, more encouraging brief notes from both Marianne Moore and the dean of modern American poetry, William Carlos Williams, who said, "an understanding of the American idiom," "excellent."

Let me requote, for the millionth time, Blanche Dubois in Tennessee Williams' masterful play *A Streetcar Named Desire*— "the kindness of strangers."

This episode concerning Ransom I believe was my introduction to dealing with the famed of the literary world. And I
was ignorant when I left Butler University. I was still unedu-
cated after hundreds of hours of instruction. But I knew at last
that what they spoke was a fact: I no longer had to wear the
O'Neillian mask of suffering and tragedy; it had slowly but
finally had etched itself into the skin of my face and the flesh
of my soul.

4 The two most important female influences on my life
were my mother, Doris, and my Aunt Jennie Sanford.
The two most influential males were of course my father,
Andrew (Andy, to his many friends), and Werner Beyer. To
this second these same four people hold a decided influence.
It was not an easy matter to shrug away the shattering phrases
of Roy Marz and Ransom, but they eventually ceased to
rankle under the skin. When I pick up the pen — as I first write
every word with a pen rather than a machine — I no longer
hear their phrases in my ear. The words I hear, the sound
advice, the right suggestions, and the encouragingly positive
criticisms are in the voice of Beyer — not a famous personage,
simply a fine human being, an adequate scholar, and a
fabulous teacher, one to appreciate for life.

It is traditional, customary with Native people, that the
small child's education be not under the guidance, in the
hands, of the biological parents. This is an insurance that
doting parents do not crush the child with love and affection,
or the opposite. In that near-perfect Native system the education of children falls to the mother's sister and the father's
brother. These sisters and brothers are physically removed
from the natal womb, but they care sufficiently to see that a
good development of spirit, mind, and body will ensure
strengths and success in adolescence and on into more mature years so that children will be a credit to the biological
family and the extended family of the clan, and will bring
honor to the tribe (band) and nation. So it was in keeping with
tradition that my mother's sister, Jennie Sanford, and my

mother's onetime best friend, Peg Greenwood, and good neighbors, Flo Graves and Etta Zeller, would become my early teachers. It was also fitting that because my father's only half brother, Eugene, lived in Canada, Werner Beyer became my surrogate father and became my guide, not only academically but beyond those stone walls. Werner accepted this burden probably without even considering the problems, and without any inkling that Native people observed such a custom. Beyer's own sons lived in Chicago with their mother, his first divorced wife. We dovetailed our needs.

I managed this arrangement with many older men who touched my younger years. Among them were my boss, the manager of Haag's Drugstore, and my first boss in Indianapolis, the manager of the Parkview Drive-In, where I worked as a carhop, serving hamburgers and milk shakes on trays fastened to car windows. Both these men were thoughtful and knew I was a struggling student at the university and, to their perceptive observations, it seemed I was a son without a concerned father, although that was not true. My father was perpetually worried that I would not make it through this rugged life, a life with fangs eager to gobble up the frail. I wasn't as effete as my father may have believed. The world was also a major teacher pushing me towards maturity and a poetic development.

5   It seems now that my father was always bringing me home. At eleven or twelve, when my parents separated and went different ways, I elected to live with my mother, though she soon abandoned me to move to Bayonne, New Jersey, during World War II. My father was informed by Peg Greenwood that she had failed in her charge or duty, and he packed me up and sent me to her. I don't think she was pleased, as by then she had her own lifestyle, drastically changed from the role of housewife and mother in Watertown. She was independent, a working woman earning solid dollars, and the mistress of her own fate. The move to Ba-

yonne, New Jersey, my mother's new life arrangement, the school I was deposited in, and the manic wildness of confused adolescence led to a grave sin on my part. I was truant from school nearly all of the 180 days of the academic year— which brought me before a juvenile court judge. He pronounced me delinquent and imposed punishment. My father appeared before the court and asked permission to take me home under his care and guidance. I stayed in his house. His home remained my home, even though at times I actually lived away from Watertown, until he died in 1957, when I was twenty-eight years old.

He saved my life twice.

Now in my father's house I was afforded time to reflect and meditate, I might say. My urge to write was a molten need. I read voraciously everything my hands touched, particularly the plays of Eugene O'Neill and Shakespeare and the poems of Robinson Jeffers and Louise Bogan.

Once I was back in a small town centered in a farming community, a community again not half so sophisticated as Indianapolis, I had the opportunity of exploring the land again. In high school I had spent much time horseback riding over what were called the State Street Hills—the western foothills of the Adirondacks. Now, no longer a high school sophomore, I wandered these hills, hiking in the spring and summer. I'm not sure what I was seeking: peace, probably; beauty, surely; and maybe to touch into some vision, some spiritual quest. When I wasn't working for my father in his business, I spent my free time on the hills, wandering, contemplating, sucking in the serene beauty. I could stand on a hill's summit and see the St. Lawrence River valley and imagine Akwesasne (St. Regis Reserve) in the very far distance, and I could view the green and blue Adirondacks with my naked eyes and through binoculars. I roamed the flowered fields, strolled the shore of the Black River, and burned away the night composing poems. Many nights my father would enter my bedroom and quietly turn out the lamp, knowing I was exhausting the mind and spirit. The hills and rivers helped heal my dark soul and damaged mind. My father's support completed this difficult task.

My writing continued, or words rather, words and rhythms, continued to pour out of my imagination through a pen. I became more confident, found new images or freshened old ones, new objects and ideas. I had something to write about, not merely wanton joys of youth, as youth was seeping figuratively through my fingers, getting away from me. I was finally growing as a writer and a man—though many have said that writers never truly resolve the man into the adult. The poet must cling to some of the trappings of youth. Where else will he find the freshness to work out of and into the poems? I listened to chicory on the winds, I smelled the ripe wild strawberries, I observed the flight of birds, especially the red-tailed hawk, which hunted the surrounding valleys and the woods of the hills.

Roy Marz had made two mistakes. He had attempted to deny my talent as a poet, to dampen the lyrical urges, although, instead of killing the snake or the hawk, he had presented a challenge. I would prove him wrong, and John Crowe Ransom as well. The second mistake Marz made was to introduce me to the poetry of both Williams and Jeffers, especially the rock-hard poems of Robinson Jeffers. Jeffers became my staff of inspiration. One poem alone brought me into the surreality of conscious dream, "Hurt Hawks":

> The broken pillar of the wing jags from the clotted shoulder,
> The wing trails like a banner in defeat.

That had been me. I was a hawk:

> He wandered over the foreland hill and returned in the
>   evening
>   asking for death,
> Not like a beggar, still eyed with the old
> Implacable arrogance. I gave him the lead gift in the twilight.
>   What fell was relaxed,
> Owl-downy, soft feminine feathers; but what
> Soared: the fierce rush: the night-herons by the river

> cried fear at its rising
> Before it was quite unsheathed from reality.

I knew from Iroquois lore, tradition, that the hawk was the messenger of the people to the spirit world. The poet was also a messenger. I became the hawk, the poet, and the messenger.

> I rise morning after morning
> And walk through the wet meadows
> Though I never frighten off the hawk
> With a gun or with a cry,
> But I have sometimes held
> It bread and bits of meat
> To coax it from the sky.
>
> His talons drip with honey,
> His beak is full of gentian leaves
> And blossoms, and his eye
> Shines with a strange kindness
> As his feathers dust the sky.
>
> What drives the babe to suck
> And kneads the blood with passion;
> What tickles idiots
> And has them laugh
> Drives my hand to clutch
> His feathers and wear
> Them in an ancient fashion.

Many years later, I dined at the home of the avant-garde poet/editor Kirby Congdon. With a gold goblet of wine in his right hand, he exclaimed that when he first read "Hawk" he learned to hate me. Smiling, of course, he added that the hatred was because I had written a marvelous poem and it had been published in my first book, *Dead Letters Sent,* and he as yet had not published a book. I was several years younger. Kirby's remark was meant to be a compliment, though he is known for crankiness. He also informed me that "Hawk" was the first contemporary Native American poem he'd ever read.

That was a delightful evening—above and beyond his kind words. At his table that night, assisting him in all his host's duties, was his companion, Ralph Simmons. Kirby had assembled a charm of a guest list. Robert Peters was visiting New York City, offering a reading of his poems at the nearby Poetry Society of America, I believe. It was our first introduction. Also at the table sat two most extraordinary women: the late Barbara Holland, and the unique Helen Adam—both poets of tremendous talents (Helen passed in 1993, aged eighty-three). I was to become closely acquainted with both these women years later. In fact, only last year my firm, Contact/II Publishing, brought out a posthumous collection of Barbara Holland's. Helen and I dined many times. I was fascinated by her and her ballads, especially the sea chanties she composed so bizarrely and craftfully.

My response to Kirby's exclamation about my "Hawk" poem was that the poem would never have been conceived, much less written down, had Robinson Jeffers not awakened me to probe not only the flight of hawks and the spirit but also death, because the poem was written thinking back to "Hurt Hawks," my school days at Butler, and the stupid attempt at suicide. Jeffers opened my eyes and spirit to image and symbol. At last I had begun to understand the incomprehensible, the magic of poems, the undiscovered, dreams, and the memories that turn into dreams as dream coats the hurt and pain in many colors. Such a hurt is so deep, so painful, that memory must bury it or we cannot survive. Bury the seed or the bulb of the wild plant so that eventually, come spring, it will rise out of the earth and blossom. My poem "Hawk" was the result of the burial of hurt, shattered illusion, fragmented dream, the broken glass in the kaleidoscope of youth, in the most tender flesh and sinew.

It is so easy to slip into maudlin sentimentality when reviving, revising, the early cracked years of one's youth, to remember too much thunder, too many roses, too much blood and hell screams. As one tries to get outside the revery, the brain's stockpile of vivid remembrances, scenes and actions never, never lost, perhaps is multiplied or saccharined by time. I might say Robinson Jeffers saved my life while Gerard

Manley Hopkins and A. E. Housman saved my soul. Wordsworth did nothing for me, but caused me to compose the
worst poems I've ever written—not that he is a bad poet, but
that I was a bad student to his poetry.

I dallied with Robert Frost and Eliot, but Frost's rhymes
stuck in my craw and continued to remind me of Ransom's
predictions. Eliot, who wrestled with his own spirit, his faith,
continued to have some effect on me, but I abandoned his
lessons because his faith led him in a different direction from
where I insisted on travelling. He had turned to Europe and
Judeo-Christian belief, and I honestly did not wish to go that
road. Jeffers (and later other writers) and my muse—for lack
of a better term—demanded I stay in this ancient world,
America, "on turtle's back." As Eliot immersed himself in
Christianity and literary criticism and French symbolism, I
moved forward into the newness of the old to revive the
ancient strengths of this land, this earth, yet, even these
waters and this sky. The winds which tapped my pen were
from the four corners, the four directions of the ruins of a
tribal society Eliot had ignored. His sails were blown by ocean
winds; mine came down off the mountains. Perhaps I clung
tighter to Frost than I thought all these years. I clung to Frost
and Robinson and a woman poet from Canada, a Mohawk
poet not as widely recognized as those gentlemen, but a
woman poet who is respected and remains in print even
though she died in semiobscurity in Vancouver, British Columbia, in 1913. E. Pauline Johnson—grandmother to Native
American poets, a Mohawk who did not renounce the Indian—survived as did Native songs and stories. She had no fear
and possessed much talent. She has remained a flag breathing in the same air as the reputable and resilient hawk, and
her work survives in a world where poetry is neither read nor
respected. Poetry is a career that receives little applause from
any nation or community because society believes it can exist
and maintain life without the heartbeat, the indomitable
spirit, of poetry. Fortunately, Johnson's literary grandchildren
have continued to pay the respect of admiration, and her

poems—though often didactic and sometimes a touch too purple—have remained stamped in printer's ink, and they stand on the bookshelf with others of her kind and breed.

We may be a vanishing crop. Our harvest does not fare well in the market today. Our society thinks—and I stress, thinks—it can do without us, although that is far from the truth. The very soul of humankind is the spirit of poetry. Without it I should have remained in the shadowy ward in the Indianapolis hospital with the black youth combing my hair over and over again, or my "pillars of the wing" would still "jag from the clotted shoulder." Poetry may have damned me, but it has proved to be my sustenance. It was my corn, the venison of my life, and I believe it is the nutrition of human life, its spirit. Without it we are doomed to petrify: ceremony will cease; a space venture to Mars will never happen; gardens will wither; children will be born old; and meadowlarks will no longer sing.

6   In the fall of 1956 I wisely registered at St. Lawrence University. I'm often amazed how sometimes I can be very bright, have enough intelligence to do the right thing, make the correct or important choice. I signed up for a survey of English literature with a professor, Douglas Angus, who I later learned was not only Canadian born but, like Roy Marz, a published author—though Angus's persuasion was fiction rather than poetry. I felt safe under his care. He would not embarrass nor hurt me by rejecting my poetic output—because I wouldn't admit I was composing poems.

I barely recall the writers we studied. I remember Wallace Stevens, William Faulkner, and oddly, Shelley, whose scientific imagery, wealthy background, devious lifestyle never had much effect on my particular needs or thoughts. Faulkner I was more acquainted with.

I was very lucky to take a course on modern fiction with the incredible and unforgettable professor Allegra Stewart, who walked into our Saturday 8:00 A.M. class in a mink coat down to her leather toes. She dripped diamonds. She was obviously wealthy, but she was also a Gertrude Stein scholar and not on tight terms with Roy Marz, who dismissed Stein as an aberration. Stewart lead me to Joyce, Lawrence, Faulkner (again), Truman Capote, Willard Motley, and others. All of those novelists remain not merely on my bookshelf but in the light of my mind.

I cannot recall exactly what Angus directed us to read of Shelley's. I know we read Frost's "The Silken Tent," which did not much attract me, and his fabulous "The Witch of Coos," which has remained a lifelong favorite. In any case, Angus asked us to write a brief paper on a Shelley poem. At the end of the class period and on the way to the door, he stopped me while I was getting into my coat—it was winter then and cold, and snow flurried outside—it was a good Frostian not Shelleyan night. "And you, young man," he said, "you can't hide from me under that bulky coat. You, young man, are a poet. And I want you to compose your essay on Shelley in verse." He started to walk off as if I had been dismissed. He has that way to this very moment when I visit his residence in Canton, New York.

Zeus himself struck me with an enormous charge of lightning. I gasped, shuddered, and began shaking. The cold night air whipped at my chin. Falling in behind him, the general, I tugged at his overcoat sleeve and stuttered that I was not a poet; that I never wrote poems. Like a train striking into a steel wall, he abruptly stopped, oblivious to the snowflakes falling around his ears and raised coat collar.

"You can't hide, my son. I know you write poems. Nearly everything you write is poetical, lyrical. I want you to compose the essay on Shelley in verse. And furthermore, I want you to bring me your poems to read." He turned, left me in the flurries of snow, flakes sticking to my eyelashes, to my warm lips, and figuratively to my leaping heart, to my joy. I'd been discovered.

The essay I wrote on Shelley was stupid, idiotic garbage. Angus expected that. He knew of what he asked. But I brought him the poems he requested, poems like "Hawk,"

"The Hopeless Kill," "Four: In the Chinese Manner," "Noon," etc. It seems now that he made no technical, written comments on the separate pages. But he did remain after class one night and discussed the work with me in person. Contradictory to Marz, he showed sincere approval for my young, raw talent. I explained Marz and Ransom's critical position; I spoke of Beyer's appreciation. He, Angus, nodded his lionlike head. Douglas Angus is a very tall, thin man. I always thought he would have made a sensational scarecrow in the *Wizard of Oz* — except his stance was stiff, unbending. Just his stance. He is a university professor to the hilt, the perfect stereotype. But obviously he also was a man of immediate concern with a rich sensibility and a heart that could reveal its warmth even in a snowstorm.

"You must continue to write poems. You are very good; have much to learn, much to live and experience; much to read, hopefully to show you the way. But you have a god-given talent. Perhaps since that other teacher examined your poems, you have developed a sensibility. Now go home and write."

Douglas Angus was a godsend, a man who saved my life.

He encouraged me away from Whitman and Frost and Eliot, and decidedly, away from Wordsworth. He gently pushed me closer to Keats, Jeffers, Williams, Hopkins, Faulkner (but that is another story), and Bogan. Edwin Arlington Robinson became important to me at this time. Dylan Thomas, so easy to poorly imitate, began a journey out of my view as though a windshield wiper's blade had wiped him off my glass bulwark. He was not to be forgotten entirely, but no longer would serve as an influence. Frost also was relegated to textbooks. His photo no longer was tacked to my studio wall so that it faced out, or down, onto where my pencils and typewriter lay — as Faulkner is tacked today.

No living human being would again hold such a powerful sway as Angus had over my poetic imagination until I entered New York University and registered to take a creative writing class under the direction of Louise Bogan. Later Willard

Motley, and later yet, Leslie Marmon Silko and Simon J. Ortiz, would emerge in my thought. But then, in 1956, I was wrapped in the congenial and yet explosive tutelage of Douglas Angus. To this day I enjoy visiting him in his Canton home; as an instructor I use his fine anthology, *The Best Short Stories of the Modern Age*—which includes the remarkable story by William Faulkner, "A Rose for Emily." He had once remarked that Faulkner was a weak writer and not worthy of a read, let alone study. I was required to write a term paper for Angus's course. I had read *As I Lay Dying*, etc., and chose to write on Faulkner—on "The Symbol as Moral." Douglas refused to give me permission, but when I protested, he finally did relent and honored my request. I believe I received an A — on the paper, but more important to me than the grade was what he wrote on the title page: "My apology. You have proven Faulkner worthy." I have often wondered if my paper had anything to do with "A Rose for Emily" being selected for his very well-received anthology, in print to this very moment.

7   I've never finished with school, with study. One doesn't. I've never truly been concerned with grades, degrees, jobs. If society says you must have them, then play the game and have them. What I was concerned with was study and knowledge that would aid me in writing not well, but greatly.

On the strength of this sense of discipline, responsibility, motivation, and drive, I Greyhounded to New York City and took the entrance exams at Columbia University—which I passed, though hardly in glowing neon. The examinations were tough, and math questions most probably lowered my overall grade. I was to enter Columbia in June of 1957. April of that year found me in the city looking for a rented room and a job. The room I found was at 66 Morton Street in West Greenwich Village, a street arched over with trees. The house was only a block away from the painting studio of the poet e.e. cummings. I stood hours, in snow and rain, watching for the great man to exit. I managed to see his shadow once or twice. I also was fortunate to see Frank Lloyd Wright during the building of his Guggenheim Museum, a masterpiece of architecture, and I managed a glimpse of Carl Sandburg strolling around the fountain in Washington Square hugging his guitar. So close was I to creativity and fame.

The job I found was as a dollar-an-hour clerk in the Marboro bookstore on East Fifty-ninth Street, not far from the Hotel Pierre on Central Park and F.A.O. Schwartz—neither of which could I ever dream of entering. I worked diligently at the "remainder book shop," and I loved my labors. My boss was generous in teaching me retail, and in no less than three months I found myself manager of the store. Needless to say, I did not enter Columbia that June. We were at the artistic pulse of the city, and many celebrities shopped with us. Not far off were Carnegie Hall and the Art Student's League. We were a few steps from the white way of the legitimate theater. The palacial movie houses lit up Broadway a half dozen blocks from the store, and so on. A favorite customer was the handsome Jeff Chandler, who, as a good Jewish actor, played many Indian roles. I remember Cochise as being one. Clerking for me was the young college-age daughter of Dr. Robert E. Rothenberg, famed as the author of the very popular book *Understanding Surgery.* She was entranced by Chandler. She was probably some five feet, five inches tall. He was broad and over six feet. The first day he entered the shop, she looked up into his face and fainted upon recognition.

It was at the Fifty-ninth Street Marboro that I hired the late American poet Asa Benveniste, of Zero Press renown. Not only was he well published and respected, but he had composed an introduction to the novel *Brothers and Sisters,* by Ivy Compton-Burnett—then a favorite writer of mine. I was thrilled to have Asa work for me. He was generous but honest in his appraisal of my own poetry, and especially of the poems that later went into *Dead Letters Sent.* No, we did not have these critical sessions while at work. Asa critiqued my poems at the old White Horse Bar in Greenwich Village, made famous first by Dylan Thomas and later by Brendan Behan, the playwright. Any night of the week, after closing time you were allowed to drink beer in a small, crowded backroom and listen to the Clancy Brothers sing out their drunken Irish hearts till dawn. I became friendly with Tom Clancy, and years later we were neighbors in Brooklyn Heights. They were marvellous singers. The women thronged to them. I believe it was Tom who gained a part in the first production of Dylan Thomas' *Under Milkwood,* and the rest, naturally, is history.

The White Horse was a bastion of fun, hilarity, and cheap beer. The melee of poets and artists was staggering. But shortly thereafter the bar lost its bohemian appeal, the Clancy brothers went off to fame, and the artsy crowd moved to the Cedar Bar on University Place. The Cedar, less known for poets, became recognized as a hangout for such painters as Larry Rivers and Jackson Pollack, though Frank O'Hara could be found there from time to time.

My service as manager of the Fifty-ninth Street Marboro was short-lived. My immediate supervisor, John Zito, informed me late one Friday of my promotion to manager of the Fifty-seventh Street Marboro, to take effect the following Monday. This shop—between Sixth and Seventh Avenues— was only a few doors from the Russian Tea Room and Carnegie Hall. Here the buds of my life began to open petal by petal, and I sprouted thorn after thorn. I spent six years in that shop bending to the rich and famous and learning the numbers and the corresponding titles in Random House's Modern Library. I swept and mopped floors, ordered books, hired and fired employees, appeased irate customers, apprehended shoplifters, soothed the ruffled feathers of the famous, paid off firemen with envelopes in the back bathroom, shelved books, dressed the front window, went to night court with thieves, and built into the store inventory an excellent collection of art books, poetry, classic and modern fiction, cookbooks, and garden how-tos for suburbanites.

I began dealing with salespeople directly from the publishers. I remember ordering twelve copies of Nabokov's hotly banned *Lolita,* for which I had customers. My boss, Fred Weitzman, the company president, received the shipment at his downtown office. Fearing a government lawsuit, he returned *Lolita* to the original publisher, Olympia Press. I'd had the same problem with Miller's *Tropic of Cancer* and Lawrence's *Lady Chatterly's Lover,* both then banned in the United States. I was not so much interested in chiding the morality of the day, but in making sales and upping my daily receipts. Mr. Weitzman was a good man and held my respect. A moral, law-abiding citizen, he also was decidedly a businessman. I was soon out of the "pornography" business. Remember, in those days Joyce's *Ulysses* was kept in the library backroom, and you were not allowed to read Edmund Wilson's *Memoirs of Hecate County.*

The Fifty-seventh Street Marboro afforded me a pretty exciting life—not because I grew rich on the salary, $75 a week, somewhat up from $1 an hour as a clerk, but because of the quality and diversity of my clerking staff and the many habitual customers, my clientele. Among the clerks who worked for me were actors (Nick Smith and Michael Hadge), painters (George Ortman, then married to the actress Carol Bavossa; and Charles Dudley, who gave me the cover drawing for my book *And Grieve, Lesbia*), photographers, and a film director (Gregory Markopolis, who recently passed in Paris). But few writers worked at the store, and none whom I remember by name. Why so few writers sought employment in a bookstore—the most likely place—I have no idea. Perhaps they worked as part-time waiters or in the libraries.

Near my desk at this moment sits a collection of short stories published first in the *New Yorker* magazine. The book was presented to me in 1960 as a Christmas gift by my staff. I read the inscription of signatures: "Nick, Ed, George, Michael, Dudley." Now I recall that Ed was a writer. All of these men were heavy readers, and I allowed them to borrow books from the stock. They couldn't afford to buy many on their meager salary of a dollar an hour, especially since most of these young men worked only part-time. They were all good men, and I remember them well, with fondness and gratitude for giving their all and being so excellent at what might have seemed a demeaning job, though in reality it wasn't. I remember saying one morning to Nick, "How is it that I never have to tell you to sweep the floor?" It was as if I had struck him aside the cheek. He reared back, studied a moment, smiled, and answered, "I couldn't stand being told to sweep the floor. I'd quit. Thank God, you never commanded me to."

To my knowledge none of those men has gained great reputation in his chosen artistic field with the exception of George Ortmen, the painter, who, a year or so after leaving the shop, showed his work at a prestigious gallery, The Stable, to huge crowds for large prices. George is indeed a most creative artist, and his creativity deserves the attention. A short, pale-faced man whose clothes were always splattered with the colors of his current work, he was a walking palette. There was always, every morning, a sweat ring around the collar of his rumpled and greyed white shirt. Marboro had a dress code, and several times I had to send him home for a tie. A nice fellow, George, but he had not much interest in selling books.

Gregory Markopolis—his death in Paris in late autumn 1992 came as a surprise. His obituary appeared on the same page of the *New York Times* as did that of my friend, the most gifted black, feminist, lesbian poet—as she was wont to say—Audre Lorde. Audre's death seemed imminent from almost the first evening we met, but still is not truly reconcilable. Tragic, tragic was the life and early death of this fabulous and generous-to-a-fault, most-democratic woman, a poet of genius. Her readings were masterful. Though we still have her intense poems, the world is darkened by her passing.

We found Gregory to be somewhat sloven and argumentative, and he carried with him an odor of grease and garlic. He was a full-blooded Greek. That doesn't mean all Greeks smell—they don't—but George did. The skin of his cheek and brow nearly always had a shine. His clothes were appropriate but not necessarily fashionable. Like Ortman, his white shirts were dingy. At the time, the staff did not consider him particularly bright. We all thought he lived in a fantasy world.

Those early years of his directorial career indicated failure to us. He was working on a film about an immigrant Greek boy crossing the ocean to America. He filmed his story on the Staten Island ferry. Money was impossible to raise. He had none, only a simple job at Marboro Books. He needed a musical score for the sound track and could not afford to hire an orchestra or obtain permission from a record company. I rented him my radio for five dollars a week so he could tape classical music. As soon as his film was completed, he disappeared from the store and my memory. I never saw him again.

Nick Smith did acquire some Off Broadway roles in various plays. One production I remember was the John Heffernan's staging of Shaw's *Androcles and the Lion.* Nick carried a spear. Mike Hadge appeared in numerous films and TV shows. Charley Dudley became night manager of a Greenwich Village bookstore on Eighth Street. Ed—whose last name escapes me—had a slight speech impediment. I have no idea what heights as a writer he may have scaled.

While managing Marboro, I met the only woman I have ever wanted to marry, and also I met my lifelong best friend.

Rose was a cinnamon-complexioned Puerto Rican woman who worked at the home office and lived with her family in the South Bronx. She was very interested in movies and the theater, and when we dated, we attended one or the other. A charming, bright, clever, gorgeous woman. She remains in my dreams. My guilts overwhelm my sleep. We should have married. My life would have been different.

British-born Wanda McCaddon I love dearly. Her magic is fetching. We traveled to Mexico together in 1962. Our journals differ so much, our recollections—well, it would be difficult to see from reading them that we had experienced the same trip at exactly the same time in the same vehicle. On our return from Mexico—which we both adored—she went west to California and entered UC Berkeley, where she became an E. M. Forster scholar, and then she taught at UC San Diego. Wanda became involved with a campus theater group, was successful, enjoyed performing, released herself from her university contract, and took off north again to Berkeley, where at this moment she continues a successful acting career. Her special magic has been the basis for numerous poems.

A couple of years ago Wanda was featured in what may possibly be the worst movie made in Hollywood, *Howard the Duck*. When I ribbed her, demanding that the cost of my ticket be returned, she said, "Joke all you want. I made money and had a star over my dressing-room door." Wanda has been very busy on stage, in films and TV commercials, and in books on tape. Recently seen in *Ishi* on HBO, she remains a loyal friend and confidant along with her husband, Julian Block, a painter and raconteur, famed for Lincoln and Civil War illustrations.

As I fell in and out of love almost overnight and was convinced that I had been burned to the core by these infatuations, my life disrupted, my dreams infested, my spirit—my very soul—crushed, I wrote hundreds of poems. I rid myself of the influence of Wordsworth, Frost, Keats, the whole Romantic gang, but held on dearly to Jeffers, Robinson, Housman, and William Carlos Williams. I even allowed Eliot to gather dust. Marz and Ransom lost. Beyer and Angus prevailed. I did publish some poems in various (some now embarrassing) reviews and in such newspapers as the *Oregonian* and the *Denver Post*. Both papers paid me one dollar. The poetic forms became more contoured, projective, imagistic, with a center pole called an object. I wrote mainly of thwarted love and sizzling passion, and sentimental lyrics of apple boughs and lilac scents. Drivel. How many peach blossoms does the peach tree need? To utterly misquote my good friend the provocative poet/playwright of *Futz* infamy, Rochelle Owens.

I believed in my craft and talent even if no one else did. Pain and raw experience devised these weak works of juvenalia and frustrated hormones. My work was not taken seriously. Le Roi Jones, now Imamu Amiri Baraka, rejected them for his Beat magazine, *Yugen*. The homely, pastoral poems of northern New York that Douglas Angus had admired no longer reared their bucolic heads. I was thriving in the delights and alchemy of New York City. I was speaking, passing words and ideas with such renowned literary figures as Gore Vidal, William Saroyan, and Muriel Rukeyser. I met with young, up-and-coming writers like the street poet Jack Micheline, Jones, Jack Kerouac, and Ed Corley, who edited *Off-Broadway,* a theater review for which I also wrote. I met and interviewed Kenneth Rexroth at the Five Spot Jazz Cafe. At Cooper Union, I heard John Ciardi read his poems. I sat beside James Baldwin in a Village restaurant; observed the great performer Jason Robards in a revival of O'Neill's *The Ice Man Cometh;* sold books to Henry Fonda, Zero Mostel, Steve Allen, Walter Chrysler, Carl VanVechten; watched Ezra Pound glance at his titles in the store I managed; spied John Steinbeck enter the Great Northern Hotel on West Fifty-seventh Street; heard Leonard Bernstein conduct rehearsals at Carnegie Hall as a guest of Jack Fischer, the concertmaster. I visited Shirley Booth in her dressing room; I spoke with Rosemary Cloony often on the telephone; knew dancers in the cast of the first *Candide,* including Frances Noble (and now I'm great friends with Margaret Roy, a singer from that same great cast). I touched the hands of Vera Zorina, Victor Mature, Sylvia Sydney, Carol Landis, and Anthony Perkins. I stood in my age, of my age, yet out of my age. Yet something was very wrong. A piece of life, of my life, was missing. As a youth I had been sure that, if I could just get the snows of northern New York off my shoulders and the grass off my tongue, I would be free and content. Life would open and welcome me. All would end happily.

Things *were* happening; look at my successes. But there was a huge black hole in the center of my existence. It would take a while longer, another decade, to discover the missing pieces to the puzzle in order to complete the picture.

During those years at Marboro Books four people entered my life. And though all have since passed to just rewards, they remain prominent in memory, and their voices whisper at the ear every time a pen is placed between two fingers. Where would I be today had their lives never intertwined with mine? had their creative spirits never fired the young poet? had their sound advice been ignored and their memory eroded by time and busy-ness? It is amazing how a single human being—nonrelated by blood—can activate the juices in a positive sense, manipulate and direct a life, form it from raw amethyst, increase it in size and beauty.

Is it the wind at the corner as you turn? Is it predestination, or is it, as Thomas Hardy suggests, "crass chance"? Who knows! Not I. But we are gloriously thankful, deleriously indebted to whatever cause or sprite entangles our lives with others! The woman you speak to in the museum, perhaps out of curiosity, eventually becomes your wife. The man with whom you share a Greyhound seat while crossing America becomes your publisher, or assassin. An accidental dial of the telephone may lead to the most bizarre events.

In 1957 I moved into a small room—not much larger than six by ten feet—in a brownstone at 66 Morton Street, Greenwich Village. I was a tenacious young poet with a head start on success. One thin book was in my pocket—*The Hopeless Kill*. It had been published privately at the *Watertown Daily Times*— in the wee hours, in the dark upstairs rooms of what was then the paper's office on Stone Street. The city editor had done the job. Four years ago John B. Johnson, publisher of the paper, was to receive a citizen's award, and I was invited to give the keynote address at the SUNY presidents' annual conference. We talked together, and he informed me that he had been aware all along of what was going on upstairs in the dark.

Now it seems like a story from Sherwood Anderson's *Winesburg, Ohio*. Here is a poet with his own thin volume in a pocket, sitting in a cramped room, a ratty dresser nearly touching the cot bed, at a window overlooking a typical New York City back garden, eating an orange, and biting a small hunk of white cheese. He's reading the French poets Paul Éluard and Guillaume Apollinaire. He's waiting to go downstairs to meet the eminent, the famous Willard Motley (whose fame has since eroded.) Motley, nearly broke, was in New York City proofing his novel *Let No Man Write My Epitaph* for

Random House. Somehow he discovered 66 Morton Street, and I came upon a letter on the hall table directed to him. An audacious lad, I pursued the letter by leaving a note under his door—which he kindly responded to, inviting me to his equally tiny room for a jam jar of cheap Chianti. Within two years of our meeting, I was living and working in his house on the outskirts of Mexico City (there is an essay dealing with Willard in this book).

Willard taught me to write every single day, not to wait for an inspiration like two sticks rubbed together producing a spark. Keep a journal, enter everything, select and write. Observation was of the utmost importance, and memory was the enemy because it could easily delude in the present, could deceive, lie, or refuse to cough up the names and numbers, incidents and experiences. Don't trust memory. Keep a notebook. Eventually, I learned to prod the memory with postcards and photos. I gave up the journal as the writing became maudlin, embarrassing, and best forgotten.

At the same time I was having these lush, rich chats with Willard—over wine in his room or tea in mine—I was studying at New York University under Louise Bogan. I consider her the most important lyric woman poet published since 1900. While I am composing—in whatever mode, poem, story, essay, letter—Miss Bogan is never far from my thoughts. She taught me to edit out—rarely to edit in or flesh out. Select, select, and select some more. This was important, but her other advice was perhaps even more to the point, and exactly what was most needed in my life and work. What on earth was I doing reading those French poets and Rilke, especially in translation? Read the Americans. There were, and are, great American voices. Do not get bogged down in the lyrical rhetoric of Whitman, the sentimentality of Benét, the thievings of Vachel Lindsay, and certainly not the apparent formlessness of Edgar Lee Masters. Exert discipline on your poems by attempting to create new forms *if* the old ones do not work for your voice. She helped me to shape my voice and gave me a better understanding of "place" than I'd had before.

Cull from the past; cull from experience; do not ignore history or art; utilize what has passed before your eyes and heart and spirit. Know who you are, where you hail from, and have some idea of where you are plotting to go, your destination as a living human being. Carry no shame for your culture, your past, or yourself. She thought of herself as being "shanty Irish," and was proud of how she had overcome this stigma—in her youth it truly had been a stigma—quite the same as being an American Indian. Miss Bogan—I still cannot write of her as "Louise"—taught me, encouraged me, to look back, to look at the fields of home, the woods and hills, the chicory and owls, the berries of the sandlots, the voices which were continually speaking, their echoes surrounding us. She taught me elegance and eloquence in the execution of these garnered images; the snow on the shovel, not just the "cherry tree," the raindrop on the earlobe. Be elegant, but simple—remember that the ordinary in the hands of the master becomes masterful. Her teachings were not too far afield from the advice of Werner Beyer. I have written of my experience as a student of Louise Bogan many times elsewhere.

A few years past, when I was a guest of the MLA Conference in New York City in 1987, I had the good fortune to sit beside and chat with Elizabeth Frank, who received the Pulitzer Prize for her magnificent biography of Miss Bogan. She appeared pleased to meet me, a former student of Bogan. At the dais for this symposium on Bogan's lyric poetry, among other scholars, sat Ruth Limmer, who had completed Bogan's pasted-together autobiography, *Journey Around My Room*, a mosaic. The session opened with Miss Bogan reciting several poems on tape. The ghost entered the room. Her strength once more overpowered me; her elegance, shy but profound, engulfed me. I was carried back to the first night in her classroom, when she readily admitted that she was not going to teach us how to write poetry. She would correct our punctuation and grammar, and we should not expect more; if we did, "then go get your tuition back" (though I may be misquoting, these many years later). Wisely, I did not go to the bursar's office for the tuition, but remained and studied.

The year of the MLA symposium was the year my selected poetry, *Between Two Rivers,* was published. I gave Miss Limmer, who was Bogan's literary executrix a signed copy. She looked surprised when I told her who I was. *Journey Around My Room* is indeed a mosaic of various writings by Miss Bogan. It deals with her life as woman and artist—though it weaves and braids with joy and depression. She was a tragic woman in my mind for all her successes, poems, and awards.

Louise Bogan brought me home, returned me to the snows and hills of northern New York. She, along with Willard Motley, had begun to shed light into that dark hole, the missing ingredient in my life. Many of the poems in my second collection, *Dead Letters Sent,* were produced under Bogan's guidance, particularly the title poem, which she admired.

Miss Bogan was in great demand on the reading/lecture circuit in those days. She frequently missed classes, but never canceled. We students were fortunate in her replacement or proctor. It was always the poet Donald Allen, editor of probably the most important and perhaps the first Beat anthology, *New American Poetry,* which remains a classic. Allen was in class the evening I was to present Miss Bogan with my poem "Dead Letters Sent." Allen read it aloud to the class and then asked me to read it. Once class was finished, we walked to the subway together. He praised the poem and exclaimed that had he read it sooner, he would have included it in his anthology. It was too late. The book was with the typesetter. His statement was a great thrill anyway.

Paddy Chayefsky was a short stout man when I first met him in the bookstore on Fifty-seventh Street. Already he had received accolades and national attention for his film *The Goddess,* the TV dramas *Marty* and *The Catered Affair,* etc., and his Broadway success, "In the Middle of the Night." He was about to receive enormous praise for another Broadway production, *The Tenth Man.* Paddy was born a Jew in New York

City in 1923, and we shared many similarities. Even though we were not far apart in age, he became a father figure for me, even while he was married and a biological father (strange, I never met his family). He lent himself to the role of my mentor, at the same time allowing and encouraging my guidance, particularly when it came to advising him on what to read.

Chayefsky blustered into the long, narrow shop out of the north wind, his dark overcoat upsetting books placed on the cash desk. He was cocky, arrogant, and yet his twinkling eyes belied meanness; instead they suggested that this was a raw gem, polishable, ready to be shaped. When he spoke, it was in a near shout, a command. Apparently he had worked sufficient years in the theater that he had acquired a directorial attitude and trained vocal chords. He was Broadway's baby at that time. His plays and TV dramas were hugely successful, so he had a right to a boisterous, demanding personality. The opposite side of his character, off stage, was that of May snow melting. (Years later, in Mexico City, I was entertained by Alma Reed, the Orozco biographer. She introduced me to Budd Shulberg, who, like Chayefsky, had that same rough exterior, but whose soul was made of lark or hummingbird feathers.)

"I'm going to Russia for the State Department with other American writers on a cultural exchange," Paddy exclaimed. Something of a thrill was mixed with his businesslike gruffness. "I need to take a collection of American authors!" My astonished face met his absolutely honest eyes. His candor suggested that he did not know American authors. "I don't mean Hemingway and the like. They know him." We spent an hour together, rattling off names and discussing various writers. At this time, memory fails to produce from the computer exact names and titles. Surely, Truman Capote, Willard Motley, Jean Stafford, and William Faulkner, who was not terribly fashionable in literary circles at that precise moment. Certainly, James Purdy's masterpiece, *Malcolm*, was suggested. (Through Motley I met Purdy when we both were living in Brooklyn Heights, years later. We bumped into each other at a secondhand bookstore and became friends. In 1986 I copublished his poetry collection *Brooklyn Branding Parlor,* off Contact/II Press.) I would certainly have advised Paddy to pack Shirley Jackson and Shirley Ann Grau's *The Black Prince,* which was enjoying a hearty success. And of course, Flannery O'Connor. The classics he knew: Hawthorne, Melville, James, Cooper, Cather, and hopefully, Crane and Wharton, though I was never exactly sure. He was a graduate of City College of New York, a reputable college. What Paddy's major was, I have no inkling. It was obvious he knew few of the leading American authors of his time other than the Hemingway gang, Steinbeck, and the playwrights: O'Neill, Miller, Williams, and so on. He appeared happy and relieved of a burden. With a handshake and a smile, he bombed out through the open door into the late winter afternoon and soon flew off to Russia. His figure disappeared from sight and mind, another demanding celebrity who knew no bounds in harassing a book clerk's brain and causing sore feet.

I had met many Hollywood actors like Chayefsky. Ralph Bellamy and Henry Fonda, for example, were of that nature; they would spend hours of your time browsing art books only to storm out of the shop without making a single purchase. Some of the famed and infamous were not always greeted with happiness and smiles. Usually the poets were more humane, understanding, even compassionate toward weary underpaid clerks. Muriel Rukeyser, who had just then published *One Life,* a biography of Wendell Wilkie, was unfailingly warm and gentle, and took time to speak of writing to a nosey poet. Many years later, after a reading of her work at the University of Buffalo, she recalled the bookshop and the many delightful chats we had. She had suffered a stroke recently and came to the stage with the help of a cane. Her poems were printed on very large plastic placards for she was going blind. Indeed, only a few months later she passed into literary history.

This meeting at UB with Rukeyser reminded me of the last concert Billie Holiday gave, at Randall Stadium in NYC, which

I attended. She was led to the microphone, which she gripped for dear life. At the end of her performance the great lady was again led off the stage to thunderous applause—even though drugs and life itself had stolen her magical voice. America has produced many startling artists, artists who have borne pain and suffering of both body and soul that may not have been displayed on their countenances. Roy Marz's writings helped me to wear that early mask.

Chayefsky returned from Russia shortly. We became acquaintances, then friends, and next I found myself in his employ. Once he was to go on safari to Africa. He invited me to travel as his companion at his expense. I declined the invitation: it sounded more like a command. He could be difficult, and anyway, I was involved in a heated affair. At the time he had been commissioned by Elizabeth Taylor to write a screenplay of the life of Edna St. Vincent Millay, in which Taylor, naturally, would star. We worked very hard on the script; Paddy diligently reporting each new scene to Miss Taylor. We finished, struggled over the title, came up with something, as I now recall, like *The Rose*. On receiving the script, Miss Taylor ignored the hard labor, even the inspired creativity, and fluffed off the work—as she, or some agent for her, decided that Millay was not worthy of her portrayal on the screen. Paddy and I were devastated, but not destroyed.

In March of 1962 I left with my friend Wanda and traveled to Mexico. I never saw or spoke with Paddy again. Occasionally I take down from the bookshelf his volumes of plays and reread inscriptions like this one: "To Maurice—without whom I would have no leisure." Paddy has since died, but he left a rich legacy. With Paddy Chayefsky I had at last placed a right foot into the literary world. There would be others to help me lift into the realm of the mystical printed word.

The great American literary critic Edmund Wilson has written that Paddy Chayefsky was "cheap, conceited, and corny." Wilson heatedly disagreed with Paddy's ideas concerning Russia and Lenin. Personally, I did not find Paddy either cheap or corny; conceited, well, I'm not so sure. We must remember that Wilson was an upper-crust literary snob—great mind though he possessed. My friendship with Paddy was another Odysseus/Telemachus experience, and I shall always remember this remarkable man with affection and pride. His skill and glamour were contagious, offering me something I had always yearned for but considered unattainable.

The West Fifty-seventh Street Marboro often seemed a literary soiree: the ambiance was breathtaking to us menial clerks—George, Nick, Charley, Mike, Ed, and I. We trembled in awe of the famous actors, writers, and painters who scurried in and out of the shop, but were too intimidated to approach them. Ralph Soyer, who taught at the Art Student's League, periodically walked our aisles. The Countess Maria von Trapp, whose life was portrayed in *The Sound of Music*, many a time leaned her elbows, in Swiss attire, on my cash desk. Katharine Hepburn came in on several evenings, but I was off duty, much to my chagrin. Sylvia Sidney came and went regularly with six or seven yapping poodles. She was sweet, but overly made-up; lipstick rather drooled from her wrinkled lips, and rouge clowned her cheeks. She was delighted that we remembered her Hollywood portrayals, and later, I was especially happy when, brought out of retirement, Miss Sidney received an Academy Award for *Summer Wishes, Winter Dreams*. Only the other night I watched a rerun of her *An Early Frost*. It was not beyond imagination that she and Henry Fonda might appear together in the store as they had starred together in *The Trail of the Lonesome Pine*, the film for which she is best remembered.

Two other women of not-so-great prominence as Silvia Sidney and Hepburn also frequented the store. A certain Mrs. Anspaucher, a most elegant lady high in years, struck up an acquaintance and would often take me to lunch. She once offered me her summer home in Connecticut, so that I could write away from the stress and bustle of city life, I believed. There were strings attached to this invitation that didn't really offend me, but rather shocked my youngish sensibilities. Mrs.

Anspaucher was very handsome—her physical beauty reminded me of Louise Bogan to a degree. She was very wealthy and always wore many large diamonds. Perhaps I missed a "golden opportunity." Later it was published that she had willed a sizeable amount of money to the Joseph Papp Theater in memory and honor of her late husband, who had been something of a playwright and poet. Mrs. Anspaucher recorded his verses as she channeled his spirit from the afterlife. She inscribed a copy of the published book to me. Rose and I declined the nefarious invitation.

Another woman, who popped into the shop late one afternoon in order to ask a question, was a "lady with a past." She had been a Hollywood film director in the mid-1950s, the time of McCarthy's terrible and tragic witch hunts. She and her husband, a TV producer, had been blacklisted as Communist sympathizers, "pinkos" as they were called. Mary Tarcia certainly had political ideas and ideals, but who didn't? To breathe in America is political, *as the bromide goes.* I have no reason to believe then, or to consider now, that Mary was a Communist. The subject never came up in any of our conversations. Nor did she ever introduce me to friends who might be "red" or "pink." But the scandal had ruined her film career, and she and her husband had returned to New York City. He resumed production of TV dramas such as *Cain's Hundreds;* Mary opened a drama studio on West Fifty-sixth Street across from the stage door of the New York State Theater, now located at Lincoln Center. Her talents and generosity were phenomenal and widely known. A strict coach, and one who dug into the very marrow of an actor's passion, she found the core of your being. She insisted that her students be working in a Broadway show, a film, a TV series, or at least singing or dancing in a club or on the concert stage. Among her students were Tina Louise *(God's Little Acre* and *Gilligan's Island),* Gower Champion (dancer/choreographer of many hit Broadway musicals), and Charlotte Rae. At that time in New York City there were many dramatic coaches. Mary certainly ranked at the top along with Stella Adler and Uta Hagen.

It did not take many visits for Mary to strike up a friendship. Her warmth and creativity overwhelmed me. Her jubilant, bubbling, intellectually stimulating, and pointed conversation was intoxicating. She nearly always dressed in black and dark purple. I thought she was a gypsy, not just a Hungarian Jew. She seemed a swirl of shawls and scarves. A tall, pale woman, she possessed the long, slim fingers of a pianist. She had a large circle of important show-business friends, and the parties in her lavish apartment glittered with stellar names of Broadway and Hollywood. The apartment, on West Seventy-second Street, was just around the corner from the famous Dakota, where I visited writers and the actor Robert Ryan from time to time. The grand galas at Mary's were intimidating for a young country man. I was usually speechless and terrified of so much as shaking hands with the famous. Mary, a true "Mother Spirit, Mother Courage," insisted that I should teach a course to be called "History of Drama: From the Greeks to Tennessee Williams." I taught this course with much pleasure for two years until I left for Mexico in 1962. Mary introduced me to the Broadway and film producer Robert Fryer and the brilliant actor José Ferrer, whom I had seen many years before on Broadway in a production of Shakespeare's *Othello* starring Paul Robson. Both Fryer and Ferrer were constantly on the lookout for fresh properties to stage. Mary, naturally, thought I should write a play for them. I read newly published novels and short-story collections and made several suggestions, none of which was pursued, to my knowledge. Thinking back now, I can be sure that I pushed Faulkner's novel *Light in August* as a potential play. Years later I was asked to write a libretto for an opera by Tom Bricetti to celebrate the opening of a new civic center in Florida. I offered *Light in August,* which was summarily dismissed as being expensive. Tom and I lost the commission, though he did set several of my poems to music for the flute. After I returned from Mexico, I never had the joy of Mary's company again; never saw her purple shawls, her smiles, or heard her staccato laughter again. One of us disappeared.

Of the thousands of people who entered the Marboro book shop in those years, the hundreds of celebrities like Eve Merriam and Anthony Perkins (who was always trying to borrow a tea bag and rarely bought the cookbook he had stood for hours reading, probably memorizing the recipes), the actors, the poets, the painters, the musicians, the play-wrights, the wealthy and important, and the handful who exerted some influence or offered a thumb of advice, one man stands out fondly in my memory as the most vivid and extraordinary individual who distinctively affected my writing, a unique literary figure of little fame but a long career, a figure who much influenced my youthful creativity and intellect. Altruistic, he was a walking library card file, the author of only one collection of poetry, now long, long out of print, *The Hermaphrodite and Other Poems* (1936). He did publish several other books, editing *Twenty-one Letters of Ambrose Pierce* and *A Round Table of Poets: James Branch Cabell.* He was a lifelong aficionado and critic of the fantasy writer H.P. Love-craft. As a young poet, he was on most intimate of terms with Hart Crane.

Samuel Loveman shuffled into the Fifty-seventh Street store one cold winter day, his large nose fiery red, his cheeks burning from the zero temperature. A tatty hat topped his balding head framed by grey-white hair. He wore baggy trousers that ruffled at the ankles, cracked shoes desperately in need of polish, and fogged glasses. Short and slightly round-shouldered, he stooped over the book counters, poked around the shelves approvingly, and passed out the door with a hand wave and a mumbled thank-you. He returned the next day to bargain for multiple copies of a certain collection of poetry that he'd spied on the table the day before. Immediately, we pushed aside the bargaining and delved into the world of poets and poems. He spoke of his own secondhand bookstore down in the West Village on Sullivan Street and said that I must visit some evening, which I soon did. It was usually inhabited by minor, mostly unknown writers. Soon invitations came to visit his apartment on upper Second

Avenue over "the sign of the fish." Through the years I returned again and again to his home, which seemed to be built of books. Except in the extremely large kitchen, piles of stacked books had consumed the seven-room flat. He lived in the kitchen, where there was a cot near the stove, a writing table near the sink, a floor lamp for light, and a bowl of fruit for refreshment. Only the indomitable Helen Adam, in her tiny apartment on East Eighty-second Street, which she shared with her sister Patricia, had such a huge and diverse collection of books assembled in such unusual places (in the oven, as legs for the dining table, etc.). Sam Loveman was and continues to be precious. I shall never forget him or the realms of books through which he guided me, all the while scattering fairy dust along the way. There was never sufficient time of an evening to explore all that his rooms and the rooms of his mind encompassed, but the exploration helped to satisfy the curiosity of a book-obsessed youth.

Sam Loveman's generosity knew no bounds. He attempted to have my poems published by his editor friends; he introduced me to living and dead authors whom I probably would not otherwise have met; he praised my work, offering substantial criticism of early poems; and he offered to write the introduction to *Dead Letters Sent,* in which he promised a healthy and successful writing career.

Sam died in August 1976, the same year that Walter Lowenfels (another helpful writer/editor) and Louis Ginsberg (Allen's poet father) passed. I have affectionately and gratefully written of Sam many times in numerous publications and in a long poem concerning the parallels he alleged between my poetry and that of Hart Crane. The latter were a fallacy: I have never been influenced by Crane, nor have I truthfully enjoyed his work. Louise Bogan told me that she had yet to finish *The Bridge* and did not feel that she had a strong understanding of its intention and meaning. Sam died alone in a New York City hospital with only a nurse and his executor at hand. I had visited him only a day or so before his last breath. Totally blind and heavily medicated, he hallucinated that I was Hart Crane and cursed me for desiring fame.

The Marboro shop on Fifty-seventh Street was a cornucopia and kaleidoscope of adventure and fantasy, an encyclopedia of dreams and wishes. My time there was a very rich six years in the life of a budding poet.

66 Morton Street offered many good times and new friends as well. At that time I met some crazy, weird, but delightful bohemian people, as well as others of a more serious, but not totally dreamless, nature. I have forgotten their names, if indeed I ever knew them. I'm only left with behaviors and characteristic eccentricities: the lady who wept and screamed all night and woke fresh and beautiful in the morning as though she had stepped out of a Hollywood musical; and the young woman who strolled through the cafes handing out red roses to young lovers—wearing only a silken slip, she wafted the scent of fine brandy, and our building super couldn't accept that she was an American black woman. People often came and went in the night at the Morton Street rooming house. You'd meet and chat with them outside the shower room one morning, and then that afternoon see them hurrying down the street suitcase in hand. Marie, the super, would be chasing behind, screaming for rent.

One person I remember well was a young African American student of journalism named Robert C. Maynard. He and his wife also lived in one room of a large, dank rooming house, not at 66 Morton but at Barrow and Fourth. It had a sink and a hot plate, and the bathroom was down a long, dark hallway. Many a night we sat on their stoop and drank cheap wine and read the poems of Edna St. Vincent Millay until dawn. Someone might hum a bar of Mozart, and we'd hold a lively discussion of Shaw's criticism of Beethoven, applaud the current revival of Lorca's *Blood Wedding,* or dissect the politics of the moment, the drug scene around the corner at Sheridan Square, the jazz at the local club, or whatever else struck our curious fancy. Those were great nights and great dawns, great sunrises. Then we'd dally off to work or school, happy with the darkness, the street patter of feet, the auto horns, and the color of our neighborhood. We hoped the Village tourists would take us for bohemians—long before LSD and long hair, free love, peace symbols, Bob Dylan, Watergate, Vietnam, Kent State, Wounded Knee, N. Scott Momaday, Madonna, computers, buy-your-own telephones, college financial aid, Marilyn Monroe's death, and dreams of Pulitzer Prizes and other awards. Even though we typed our papers on manual typewriters, and there were no microwave ovens, Burger Kings, or Pizza Huts, we had time to write and talk and dream. Our conditioning was Spam and hard rolls with crackling crusts. Hamburgers were rare, and steak was beyond our comprehension, let alone suits from Alexander's or Macy's. Books were secondhand from the shop on Sheridan; plays were Off Broadway. Who cared? We were young; we had Bach, O'Neill, Miller, and Mistral. We had poetry readings in the cafes, the Museum of Modern Art, the Met. We could watch Wright erect the Guggenheim on Fifth Avenue; we had evenings with guitars in Washington Square. There were forbidden moonlight swims in the pool behind the Varick Street library (where I gave my first public reading).

We had every right to fancy ourselves poets, artists, journalists, young lovers, and cosmopolitan intellects. We were the eggheads, an expression now long out of fashion. We sought other heads equal to our own. George Bernard Shaw was an icon. Truman Capote was revered, as was Carson McCullers and Garcia Lorca. We were poor but elegant snobs, poor as the proverbial church mouse, naked as the Emperor, colorful as Joseph's coat. We wanted for nothing, and nothing was wanting. Spam and peanut butter every night was fine as long as there was a ninety-cent bottle of red wine to wash it down. And we argued the quality of those cheap wines from Spain! We ate pans of macaroni doused with oleo and parsley. We "stooped" the Village and punned about the tourists who strolled by rubbernecking our lives.

One day my two friends announced that they were moving to a larger apartment in Brooklyn Heights, near Crane's glorious, enigmatic, mysterious bridge. I did manage one trek by subway to their new place. Then they vanished, and Wanda and I disappeared into Mexico. The next time I saw Robert C. Maynard he was guesting on the David Brinkley Sunday morning show. Bob had risen above the Spam and Chianti, the hot plate and manual typewriter. He had become editor and publisher of the *Oakland* (Calif.) *Tribune,* was enjoying prestige and obviously a fine salary. He no longer wore sweaters missing the elbows, but a jacket and tie. I suspected that he no longer slouched along the street, for there he sat, proud and straight in a director's chair, discussing the political problems of the world with important people. I was so proud of him and wondered if he would remember my poems. I was saddened to read of his untimely death just this last summer.

Through the years, many of my fellow workers at Marboro and acquaintances from the West Village have revisited me on the TV screen. Not only Bob Maynard and Mike Hadge but also Allan Miller has had starring roles in various dramas. Alice Ghostly has gone on to great and well-deserved fame; the actor G. Wood has made many films; Carol Channing also had come to my apartment, with Joan Lorring, long ago when I lived with David Forest on lower Park Avenue. David knew everyone in show biz and introduced me around. What a wonderful thing television is for me! It rings out the new and rings back the old, a veritable storehouse of memories. I think that the friends and students who now feed at my kitchen table must think me daffy as I go on about the old friends from my youth who occasionally pass across the screen. They suspect my credibility and patronize my memory as though I had imagined these noted people, conjured them out of fantasy.

In the early to mid-sixties I lived in Mexico and the U.S. Virgin Islands. It was there I met Tram Comb, the poet who introduced me to Florence Williams, widow of Dr. Williams. Though aging, Mrs. Williams was a real charmer. It was a sheer delight to meet her, press her hand, and talk with her. In

Charlotte Amalie, where I lived in Cha Cha Town near the Russian mansion (then in tatters and rubble) were the summer homes of many wealthy continentals. Herman Wouk also lived and wrote there. One of his novels, *The Carnival,* deals with St. Thomas and Charlotte Amalie.

In May 1966 I flew from the Islands to Chicago, where I took a job with the *Chicago Sun-Times.* There, for exactly one year, I wrote obituaries. Having discovered Chicago to be cold, unfriendly, and provincial, I proceeded to Greyhound to Brooklyn Heights, where I found a one-room studio on the fifth floor of an old brownstone for sixty-five dollars a month. I filled the room with bright colors: magentas, cobalts, acid greens, melon, and lemon, — the colors I had grown to love in Mexico and the Caribbean. Moving only once, into the brownstone next door, I lived in Brooklyn for twenty years. The last two years of my stay I began the transition to Saranac Lake in the Adirondacks. There I was hired as a poet-in-residence, but soon added additional courses in the humanities, such as North Country Literature and Iroquois History and Culture.

8   I believe it was 1970 when I became involved in owning some apartments in Chicago with a long-standing friend, Joaquin Perez. Joaquin, better known as Quino, was a merchant mariner and consequently out of Chicago on the high seas much of the time. I was elected to perform the landlord duties: to collect rents when possible and before checks got to the local tavern, to exterminate cockroaches, to paint walls, to buy hot-water heaters, to mow lawns, to solve arguments or disputes among the buildings' tenants, and naturally, to keep the five apartments rented. The buildings — there were two — nestled within a changing blue-collar neighborhood. Slowly Hispanics were moving in, and guitars, cha-cha-cha, it and the rhythms of the salsa colored the air.

I flew to Chicago once a month. On one of my flights to the windy city, in the airport and without a book for the flight home to Brooklyn Heights, I made a purchase at the terminal newstand: Mari Sandoz's *Cheyenne Autumn,* an American epic. Now, much tattered and well thumbed, the same copy remains in my possession, and within the leaves rests a postcard depicting the young, brash, notoriously confident (to the point of possible mental disorder) George Armstrong Custer. The photo was taken of the young general a year before his demise in 1876 at the Little Big Horn. The card had been sent by my good friend, and a publisher of my work, Frank Parman, who this moment carries the history of Oklahoma in his mind, a burden that one day he must put down between the covers of a gigantic and authentic book.

Cheyenne Autumn is the history of 278 Northern Cheyenne men, women, and children who despite the duress of winter broke out of their Fort Robinson, Nebraska, prison in 1878 to escape north to their homelands on the Yellowstone River in Montana. They had been ravaged in the freezing barracks by starvation, acute illness, hopelessness, loss of spirit and their lost freedom, and by the false promises of the government that they might be allowed to return home. Under the bitterest of conditions they fled the fort, and under heavy army calvary fire they crawled north across the plains in biting winds. Nearly half of these Cheyennes died by gunfire or exposure. Theirs was truly an American epic; their band was led by two mighty and sensitive chiefs, Little Wolf and Dull Knife, heroes to this moment.

Truly, tears stained my cheeks throughout the flight into La Guardia Airport, and those tears continue to fall to this very hour, especially as I sit on my mountain hillside observing the winds of March whip a snowstorm before my eyes, reminding me of the Cheyennes' heroic escape and their horrendous march home under the most grueling conditions. *Cheyenne Autumn* led me to many other books by Mari Sandoz: *Old Jules, The Battle of the Little Big Horn, The Buffalo Hunters, The Beaver Men, Love Song of the Plains,* and her masterpiece, *Crazy Horse,* the biography of the great Lakota leader, a man of mystery but also a man of heroic proportions.

Sandoz led me to other books, histories particularly concerned with the Cheyenne's, especially the Southern Cheyennes now at home in western Oklahoma. In *Cheyenne Autumn* Sandoz introduces a young Cheyenne woman, Monahsetah, and her son, Yellow Swallow, with the strong suggestion that this sickly lad had been fathered by G.A. Custer during his winter campaign against the Cheyennes in 1868 leading to his dawn attack upon a peaceful band of Cheyennes under the leadership of the peace chief Black Kettle. I spent the next five years researching this allegation with the intent of writing Monahsetah's biography and including proof that Custer sired the young Yellow Swallow, who died on the journey north to Nebraska. I wrote the book essay by essay, but when it was nearly complete, I was forced to abandon my labors: I could not locate the essential facts.

If both Werner Beyer and Louise Bogan had pointed to the road home, then surely Mari Sandoz, whom I never had the good fortune to meet, produced the vehicle in which to ride there.

The flight from Chicago to Brooklyn, the reading of that epic (as valid as any ancient Greek tragedy or martyrdom of Christians slaughtered in the Roman coliseum by pagans), the tears that have remained, the stain that is on my cheeks, all brought me home. Truly it was time as a poet to forget John Crowe Ransom, Eliot, Frost, yes, even William Carlos Williams, Jeffers, and Miss Bogan herself, and become myself. The dark was lifting, but the abyss I had been facing all my life was close, its great hole filling with history, culture, past deprivation, loneness, pain, and hostility. I had dug into all that with a fine lyric spade that would open veins of purple blood, songs aching for rememberance, and the collective memory, to misquote Carl Jung, of thousands of years of Native glory and survival, as well as the horror and brutality of the invasion and division by conquistadors who were not simpatico with any man or woman of copper skin, with any who hung a feather at the ear and danced upon the drum of earth. The Native societies were of the utmost sophistication, with workable and working governments, educational systems and scientific minds, and the ceremonial rituals and profound spirituality of their enduring religions. The greedy invaders of these lands "on turtle's shell," the thirteen ribs, had not yet conceived such civilizations. Thousands of years of prayer, song, and story were the central pole of the various and magnificent cultures that were soon to near perish from the human collective memory despite the "usefulness" of the vanishing race. The invader was not totally successful in wiping out, extinguishing, these resilient societies. The magic of written words, by such gallant spirits as Mari Sandoz, kept them alive, and the people took nourishment and reproduced until now indigenous peoples are once more gaining strength and population, pride and dignity about who they were and who they are.

Now that I rode in a vehicle home, I consumed a new alphabet and language; new words, paragraphs, books, tomes, and rites.

1969 saw the occupation of Alcatraz Island, where the government forced abandonment of the old prison. In 1973–74 the tragic confrontation broke out near Pine Ridge at Wounded Knee. Again people were murdered, and some simply disappeared forever from human eyes. Others again were forced into jails, freedom and spirit denied. Though I was not present at Wounded Knee in the church, shelled by government bullets, because I had a heart attack that June, my mind and spirit took a position in that church. When I regained a semblance of health, I returned north to the Saint Lawrence River valley—to Akwesasne, St. Regis Reserve, home of the Mohawks, the eastern branch of the Haudenosaunee—to work with the various minds and hands producing the important journal *Akwesasne Notes*, then edited by Jerry Gamble, a Jewish man of excellent mind and intelligence, who had been adopted into the Mohawk Nation because of his depth of concern, his knowledge, and his labors on behalf of not only Mohawks and Iroquois but also Native people across North America. It was while living in Nation House that I composed the poems for *Dancing Back*

Strong the Nation. I was sleeping in a room actually held by Mohawk poet Alex (Karaniaktatie) Jacobs, who was off attending university in Canada at the time. Peter Blue Cloud, poet, trickster, storyteller, and editor, was then poetry editor of *Notes,* and Daniel Thompson, poet and artist, was also there sharing mugs of Indian tea with me. I helped Peter sort out the poems to be printed in *Notes.* I wrote bits and pieces of book reviews. Generally I tried to make myself useful when I wasn't working on the poems for the collection. *North: Poems of Home* had already appeared via *Blue Cloud Quarterly* under the editorship of Brother Benet Tweden, who was making a tremendous impact on Native and American literature. (I'm not sure that there really is a division between the two, especially if one thinks that American history is Native history and vice versa.) Brother Benet was printing chapbook after chapbook by Native writers, at huge financial losses, I'm sure — Wendy Rose, Duane Niatum, songs of Buffy St. Marie, and so on — making visible what was then utterly invisible.

9 My father was born in 1900, not a time in America, let alone in northern New York state, to shout, "Hey, I'm an Indian." At fourteen or fifteen he left Canada and took up residence in Watertown, New York, where he gained employment with the Water Department. His job was to carry the water bucket to the workers, to men who were digging new lines. He had only two years of schooling, through what he called "the Second Book," or the second grade. He could — with hesitation — read and write. He was a hard worker, industrious, and serious, and by the time I was born he had been made foreman. When he died in 1957 he was either the proprietor or the lessee of three gas stations and a restaurant. He was continuously ill the last five years of his life, but this illness did not hinder him from building a new home, in which he lived only one year. While foreman for the Water Department, he had been in a position to hire and fire work gangs doing minor jobs. He had hired many immigrant

Italians who could not speak the language but were married to marvelous cooks, and he often partook of rich pastas and richer red "dago" wine.

My father also hired many Native men who had come down from Kanawake near Montreal or from Akwesasne. My father was always a just and generous man, though there were times when, as a high school youth, I questioned his ethics. He became political, and it was not beneath him to ask political favors with a quart of bourbon in his hands. These Native men who came to Watertown seeking work with their wives and children naturally needed homes. My father was in the position to help, and he did. The city owned several houses, and somehow these houses came under the jurisdiction of the Water Department. Of course, my father saw that the Natives were given the houses. Rent in those days was something like five dollars a month. As a lad he had received fifty cents a day for his labors. Later, salaries increased, but not by much. Those were the depression years.

Though he aided the Native families, and several families were holed up in housing near the house in which my family lived, my father cautioned me not to play with the children. He gave no reason. His word was the law, though I was often discovered breaking that law. As a small child my father rarely spoke of his Indian heritage because of the stigma. He would tell stories or sing songs without identifying the source. He told the stories as though he had just simply used his imagination and had at that precise moment invented the tale or the song. Yet he was teaching, and he meant to teach. He meant that I would learn these stories, though I'm not sure he anticipated my using the tales years later in poems that I would write. I don't think he had any idea that I would become a writer. It wasn't until I entered high school that I really showed much artistic interest. I painted, but not well. I sang, but shyly. I wrote many poems and stories but this writing showed little talent, I'm sure. I did write many, many letters to the editor or the *Watertown Daily Times*. In high school I was busy riding horses, working for my father, attending weekend teenage dances at the school or YMCA, camping and swimming.

As I grew older, an adolescent, my father talked more and more of his own boyhood, and more often told stories concerning his own blood mother. He never ignored his Irish father and spoke many times of Irish relatives still living in Ireland, but his Irish ancestry was never pushed too hard, though I remember once he said that at school, if a teacher asked what my nationality was, I was to tell them that I was Irish and English—my mother was English and Seneca. He said it would make for a better understanding—to paraphrase. Few high school lads have solid relationships with their fathers. I was no different from any other. I believed my father to be obsessively conventional, tough, restrictive. Thinking back now, I see that he wasn't as tough as I then believed. He was permissive with the exception that I was to rise early in the morning, and when not in school, I had to work in either his gas station or his restaurant. This he did demand of me. He was teaching a work ethic, trying to give me a business sense, a saving-for-a-rainy-day attitude, and he prompted or persuaded me to think in terms of a business career. Should I go to college, then I should become a business major. What I did in my spare time, such as writing or painting, or even singing, well, that could be the reward for being smartly industrious and a good businessman. My father was no different from most fathers. His life had been hard, with a fraction of an education, and he wanted to insure that mine would be easier. I, of course, did not think that way, but the opposite. Let the future take care of the future. It would in all likelihood happen anyway.

My father was a hunter, a fisherman, an outdoor man. I went most always on his fishing trips; I rarely got to go hunting with him. That was probably due to interference by my mother. She was afraid of guns. She hated cleaning the rabbits or pheasants he would bring home in his game bag. She also hated cleaning the fish he brought home on the string. She complied reluctantly. He talked hunting with me.

Talked about his hound dogs. The smells of his rifles, his hunting boots, and his outerwear were always in the house. I always knew that his guns were stored in a closet in my parents' bedroom. It was never locked. I had access to it, but his teachings were strong, and I never had the desire to take the guns out of the closet and play with them. He did ask me to help clean and oil the guns from time to time. And he would tell hunting stories, and they were not stories of how the largest rabbit in the woods got away, or how the bear pulled the gun out of his hands and whacked him across the head. He never hunted bear. He never shot a bear. He held a distinct aversion—but that is not the correct word—for bear. No, no, no. He had not an aversion but a reverence for bear.

Bear is a mighty animal, not merely for physical strength, but mighty in tradition, medicine. Bear was a relative: you do not kill or eat your brother, nor walk on his fur-rug back. Bear is a mystery, spirit, legend; it is the unknown, it is the poetic. Perhaps not as noble a beast as Wolf, Bear is not without nobility in the animal world, which includes the human species. Bear is the enigma of the woods—not of the wilderness, because there is no such thing as wilderness. The wild is in the human spirit and human mind, and Bear is wildness. When Bear is extinct, then the woods are forever gone. Then the darkness, the shadows, the voices, the healing powers, the medicines of the woods will be lost into the past, the time of the past. Culture will be doomed. Bear's flesh should never be eaten, nor should his spirit be desecrated by making Bear a wall decoration or a rug before a fireplace. To wear a robe about one's shoulders made of a bear found dead on the forest floor of natural causes is and will be a compliment, an honor to the Bear, but to step on his back with dirty boots is an abominable idea. Bear is the last freedom. His extinction would be the most horrible of tragedies. Bear is the symbol of humanism, not the untamed or conquerable wilderness.

The Wolf, though he is in great jeopardy by the foolishness of Man, has at least some semblance of immortality in that he is the grandfather of Coyote and of the common domesticated house or lap dog. He will continue to be hunted and slaughtered because Man hates him and fears his fangs, and because historically he has competed with Man for sustenance, food. I believe there is a gene in the European that insists upon ridding the world of Wolf. Yet humans can learn how to live from Wolf, how to live with one another without genocidal wars caused by religions and overbreeding.

My father taught respect for bear and wolf, but he also taught respect for wild iris, or blue flag, for trillium and cattail. He taught respect for corn, berries, water, the winds. He knew their strengths. The wild iris renews the premise and promise of beauty and poetry, the song that abounds around us, that circles our natures and is a reminder of that great green ceremony of which the Lakota holy man Black Elk spoke so graciously and wisely: the green ceremony of everyday is to lift the head from the pillow and see the beauties and gifts of the day, and to be thankful.

I have no doubt whatsoever that the greatest influence on my life, actions, and thinking was given me by my father. He encouraged me in all ways, and not only to accumulate goods and monies, but to stop, half in the countinghouse, and observe the minute things of life: the ant crawling across the cabbage leaf, the tremolo of the loon, the birth of the blossom, the wheeling of the hawk in the sky, the sweet, good smell of the wild strawberry laden with mystery in the sun-drenched field or along the shady path. He was a hunter of flesh, and I became the hunter of words, but he was the first teacher. He taught me how to prepare the gun, how to keep it in good shape, how to fire and what to fire it upon. How different a man, a human, I would be had my father been any other than who he was. If I write poems or short stories, and if I write them well, it is to show him, perhaps to prove to him, that I have become a bad business person who spends no time at all in the countinghouse, but I have become a hunter and bring home to the door honors of the hunter as the hunter of words, of language.

Sandoz watered seeds of history in my thinking that my

father had planted. History itself had planted seeds—some were weeds that needed hoeing and pruning. Over years of reading Sandoz, her ideas led me from studies of the Cheyenne and the Lakota to my own Iroquois. I consulted with my Aunt Jennie Sanford, and she explained the Parker connection; we were related to the famous Seneca leaders, though no one in recent times had pursued this blood tie. My mother seemed either ignorant of it, or simply had no interest, no concern; she refused to speak of it. As my father had died in 1957, it was impossible for me to speak with him. But Aunt Jennie, the family historian, holds in her possession a very old Bible, which, honestly, I have not seen for years. It contains births and deaths covering many, many decades. The Jefferson County Historical Museum also contains a decent archive.

I knew stories, but I did not know history. Consequently I began asking questions, listening, and reading. Dan Thompson and Ray and John Fadden offered many answers. I read Arthur Parker and Henry Lewis Morgan and studied how the people of the Long House, the Haudenosaunee, formed our sophisticated culture; how government was created, mainly through the good message of the Peacemaker, Deganawidah. I made a study of the creation story and contemplated the mysteries, the magic or medicine of these everlasting stories, which, indeed, are a narrative history of the Iroquois. The more I listened and read and thoughtfully considered, the more I observed and understood. Slowly my father's wisdom, his thoughts, and his stories began to make intelligent sense; his whys or why nots of doing such or such not, thus or thus. His code of life became evident; his humanism was clear; his respect for the smallest or largest creature became understandable. I fully understood, for example, why food should not be wasted: it is the flesh of a thing once living that has given up life that we—that I—may live in good health. Not only were the scales pealing away from my sight, but the darkness of ignorance slowly receded like the tide of Lake Ontario. As a boy I had always talked with trees, particularly the black willow; with fish especially rainbow trout, which swam in the creek that flowed by my father's house; with birds, specifically the hawk, the messenger to the spirit world. Hawk became my fetish, as did the woodchuck. As an adolescent I witnessed a woodchuck's death in the green fields of spring, watching as others, who prized its tail to swing from a hat rim, kill it for an ornament. This, my father taught, was wrong.

Things somehow began to fit in place: Bogan and Beyer's suggestions that I needed to go home out of the darkness, the abyss. Peter Blue Cloud often advised me to get out of that city, New York, and go north where real life was happening. Even the Cheyenne poet Lance Henson said, on visiting me in New York City, that he couldn't understand how any self-respecting Mohawk could live in a place like Brooklyn. But I told him many Mohawks lived in Brooklyn, not failing to mention that many New York structures of high steel and iron were erected by Iroquois men.

Barbara Cameron, Randy Burns, and Sharol Graves were three young Native students: Barbara, Lakota; Randy, Paiute; Sharol, Crow. Barbara was a writer; Randy, heading towards a law degree; Sharol, both an artist and dancer. Three young, beautiful people centered in their cultures, eager to contribute, to give back to their cultures as they had been gifted with so much. We met through a newspaper advertisement. A world opened, and a prism of light and color pervaded this world. Barb and Sharol were students at Mills College; Randy was at San Francisco State, studying at that time with Paula Gunn Allen. The three had a radio program on a local radio station in the city, *Red Voices.* I read poems with them over the air many times. Randy introduced me to Paula at lunch on campus. I had been publishing poems in *Akwesasne Notes,* and Walter Lowenfels had published a poem of mine in his seminal anthology, *From the Belly of the Shark.* That poem had been submitted for me by Karoniatate: (Alex Jacobs). Paula had some idea who I was, and we formed a friendship. She introduced me to many writers in the Bay area and, later, in the Albuquerque region, mostly native writers. Through Paula and her sister, Carol Lee Sanchez, I was positioned to meet two of my heros, Simon Ortiz and Wendy Rose. Shortly after, I made friends with Janet Campbell-Hale and Mary Tall Mountain.

In those days there weren't that many Native writers who were published. We were friends and helped each other by suggesting publications and readings. We shared what little was out there. Many a time a mug of coffee was all we received for a half-hour reading of our poems. Honorariums were insignificantly small. We were excited, thrilled, just to stand at a podium with an audience, its collective head bent in concentration on our songs and chants, our stories and histories. I am greatly indebted to Barbara, Randy, Sharol, and of course Paula. I had entered a community where I belonged. The feeling of being a real poet was invigorating. Apart from being published, I was in a circle, a sacred circle of life with like kind, my own kind, native poets. I was no more the loner, the outlaw, nor even the delinquent.

Wendy Rose, Arthur Murata (Wendy's husband now), and I became three peas in a pod. I thought of her as the "Little Sister." In turn she referred to me as her "Big Brother." Considerable years of age separate us, and I am forever thankful that Wendy didn't refer to me as "Father." As time went on, I was fortunate to meet other writers with whom I became good if not fast friends: Duane Niatum, Joseph Bruchac, Diane Burns, Joy Harjo, Linda Hogan, the late Diane Decorah, Geary Hobson, Lance Henson—all Native writers. I enjoyed their beauty and talents. To this moment I hold these good people, all powerful writers, in a good light, in high regard, and I am utterly thankful that they entered my life. Simon Ortiz and Leslie Marmon Silko, if any of my contemporaries have an influence on my work, certainly hold me in the palms of their hands. Their poems and songs, their rhythms and metaphors, their ideas, were strong inducements to my own spirit and an inspiration. They became heros, and I was nearly tongue-tied when we first met and shared talk and stories. I was absolutely excited by Wendy's lyric voice and also Peter Blue Cloud's vision. I was deeply impressed with Peter's study of the river spirit, of the ripening and flight of the milkweed pod. These two writers cannot but leave at least a shadow on the poetry in English of this time. Duane Niatum and Geary Hobson, long-standing warm friends, gave me incredible support, and to this moment I feel guilty for never having given back what they offered me. Many contemporary poets have loaned me their hand, and certainly their written words, or have helped me to develop and maintain faith in my work during some very dark hours. I am obliged never to forget Dan (Rokwaho) Thompson, artist, poet, and thinker, who, over many mugs of coffee and billows of cigarette smoke, shared his thoughts late into the summer night or in winter letters. Now, years later, I still listen when we meet for coffee and cigarettes.

Four non-Native writers have pursuaded my pen and brain over the last twenty years, and they too are heros: Jim Ruppert, Rochelle Ratner, Michael Castro, and the huggable "Beaver," Jerry Rothenberg. I desired their approval so much. Hopefully, I have gained it.

Hundreds of other people over the decades have touched and colored my life and writings, and I am grateful and also a better person for their ceremonies, their care, and the intellectual relationships we have had and, with many, that we still have. What would my erratic life have amounted to without those pillars of friendship, guidance, and strength—"the kindness of strangers." I am little more than a collection, a collage, of their ideas and images; their faith and spirit have led me to emulate them as I once wished to emulate G. M. Hopkins, Robinson Jeffers, and yes, even William Wordsworth.

For many years I have firmly believed and have often spoke of the fact that my cat of fourteen years tempered my anger and rage. Sula would not tolerate violence, and I was of a violent, passionate nature. Nothing was grey. Most people would think it idiotic to believe a cat could lead you to self-awareness where a trained therapist may have failed, or a parent or friend might not have succeeded. We learn from listening. The bee teaches, the river teaches, the sun and the moon teach, humans teach, and we in turn consider, digest, separate, and gain self-knowledge by teaching ourselves; if we are fortunate, we come to our state of "bliss," as Joseph Campbell might say. We are obliged to be part of a community, an active member of society. Creating poetry and my lifelong friends have opened a crack or a link in the community circle; they have allowed me to enter and find a useful place.

This is the magic of life: the touching of hands to minds. Mystery abounds: it is on each elm leaf, each bear claw, every petal of every trillium; on the bones of our ancestors and in each drop of sperm, each egg, of all species. The mystery of creation: should we ever discover its truth, we will lose interest and die of ennui. This is why we continue seeking the new hand, why we take another hike into the mountains, a canoe trip down the river, read one more poem, and listen to another story. To touch into this great mystery—to study the mountain or river spirit, as Peter Blue Cloud might suggest— is life. Only the Creator is perfect; only the Creator makes no mistakes. Only the Creator—or as Paula Gunn Allen has written, the Creatrix—knows what is at the center—the why's—of that mystery. In the quest for vision the poet is there at the edge of the maple stand, the precipice above the stone quarry, the peak of the mountain. Poetry is the richness and magic of imagination. We do not live to our fullest potential without it. Not university degrees, nor the counting house, nor the bank deposit can ever show the open link into the center of mystery, life. Watch a milkweed seed's flight, or the dandelion; observe the butterfly shake out of its cocoon or the frog drop its tadpole tail and fins.

10 We are rounding the circle; the ceremony is green; the song vibrates; the wolf is not extinct; the story continues; the poem is yet to be dotted with the finality of a period;

spirit is strong; the leg and hand remain firm; and the memory is vivid, rich, luxuriant with the details of too many stories, of stories too long to relate here and now at this moment.

Two years ago a fine young poet/editor, Jason Shinder, invited me to submit some new poems for an anthology Harcourt Brace was to publish. The collection was titled *More Light: Father and Daughter Poems, a Twentieth-Century American Selection.* Shinder extended the definition of father and daughter. I have not sired a biological daughter or son, yet he accepted a poem from my persona book, *Tekonwatonti: Molly Brant,* a poem in Molly's voice addressing the father of the United States, George Washington, who was known to Iroquois people as "Town Destroyer." Molly is asking that the father of the new country allow the people of the Iroquois their culture, and that he not forget where the founders discovered the forms of the American government, which was based on the "good message" of the Peacemaker, Deganawi-dah. Naturally, I was quite pleased to be included in this important book, published by a highly respected press, in which were poems not only by many living friends and passing aquaintances but also by the very poets who had in one way or another influenced or touched my early work: T. S. Eliot, Muriel Rukeyser, Laura (Jackson) Riding, Amiri Baraka (who failed to see merit in my early poems, though since we have taken hands in friendship), Audre Lorde, Marilyn Hacker, and even John Crowe Ransom, who as editor of the *Kenyon Review* had discouraged me from writing verse and had broken my young heart, but not my spirit. What a surprise, a sheer delight! I have always held that revenge is coated not with cane sugar but with the traditional natural sweetener, maple syrup. Figuratively, I danced around the painted war post. I did sing, and I spoke with Ray Marz, who is now in the spirit world, and again profusely thanked Louise Bogan, Werner Beyer, Douglas Angus, and all the others who gave me support and helped rekindle faith in my own creative powers. And yes, I must thank both Ransom and Marz again for the huge part they played in my development. Without their warnings I might have become a business major as my father advised to help stay hunger from the door.

We are rounding the circle; the ceremony is green; the links of the circle have been formed by so many hands and minds. When I left Butler University in 1956, Werner Beyer said I had been a wild weed that changed into a flower. I hope he was thinking of the blood-red trillium of the northern woods and the Adirondack Mountains, endangered but resilient.

The sacred circle of life, the mathematical points, are coming together: the roundness of the whole, the fullness of life for which I am very thankful.

Adowe.

PART TWO

POETRY

THE HAWK
For Asa

I rise morning after morning
And walk the wet meadows
Though I never frighten off the hawk
With a gun or with a cry,
But I have sometimes held
It bread and bits of meat
To coax if from the sky.

His talons drip with honey,
His beak is full of gentian leaves
And blossoms, and his eye
Shines with a strange kindness
As his feathers dust the sky.

What drives the babe to suck
And kneads the blood with passion;
What tickles idiots
And has them laugh
Drives my hands to clutch
His feathers and wear
Them in an ancient fashion.

FIRST RULE

stones must form a circle first not a wall
open so that it may expand
to take in new grass and hills
tall pines and a river
expand as sun on weeds, an elm, robins;
the prime importance is to circle stones
where footsteps are erased by winds
assured old men and wolves sleep
where children play games

catch snowflakes if they wish;
words cannot be spoken first

as summer turns spring
caterpillars into butterflies
new stones will be found for the circle;
it will ripple out a pool
grown from the touch
of a water spider's wing
words cannot be spoken first

that is the way to start
with a stones forming a wide circle
marsh marigolds in bloom
hawks hunting mice
boys climbing hills
to sit under the sun to dream
of eagle wings and antelope;
words cannot be spoken first

GOING HOME

The book lay unread in my lap
snow gathered at the window
from Brooklyn it was a long ride
the Greyhound followed the plow
from Syracuse to Watertown
to country cheese and maples
tired rivers and closed paper mills
home to gossipy aunts . . .
their dandelions and pregnant cats . . .
home to cedars and fields of boulders
cold graves under willow and pine
home from Brooklyn to the reservation
that was not home
to songs I could not sing
to dances I could not dance

from Brooklyn bars and ghetto rats
to steaming horses stomping frozen earth
barns and privies lost in blizzards
home to a Nation, Mohawk
to faces I did not know
and hands which did not recognize me
to names and doors
my father shut

IN MY SIXTH AUGUST

My father wades the morning river
tangled in colors of the dawn.
He drags a net through the cold
waters; he spits tobacco juice,
stumbles. Light warns the minnows
that hide under bullheads. Sharp air
smells of wild lobelia and apple.

In my sixth August a kingfisher
rattles from a willow; I am too
busy picking iris in the wet fields
to know a game warden shakes his head
above us on the narrow bridge to home.
The west wind has trapped our scent
and light prisons our mobile hands.

WILD STRAWBERRY
For Helene

And I rode the Greyhound down to Brooklyn
where I sit now eating woody strawberries
grown on the backs of Mexican farmers
imported from the fields of their hands,
juices without color or sweetness

my wild blood berries of spring meadows
sucked by June bees and protected by hawks
have stained my face and honeyed
my tongue . . . healed the sorrow in my flesh

vines crawl across the grassy floor
of the north, scatter to the world
seeking the light of the sun and innocent
tap of the rain to feed the roots
and bud small white flowers that in June
will burst fruit and announce spring
when wolf will drop winter fur
and wrens will break the egg

my blood, blood berries that brought laughter
and the ache in the stooped back that vied
with dandelions for the plucking,
and the wines nourished our youth and heralded
iris, corn and summer melon

we fought bluebirds for the seeds,
armed against garter snakes, field mice;
won the battle with the burning sun
which blinded our eyes and froze our hands
to the vines and the earth where knees knelt
and we laughed in the morning dew like worms
and grubs; we scented age and wisdom

my mother wrapped the wounds of the world
with a sassafras poultice and we ate
wild berries with their juices running
down the roots of our mouths and our joy

I sit here in Brooklyn eating Mexican
berries which I did not pick, nor do
I know the hands which did, nor their stories . . .
January snow falls, listen . . .

BOSTON TEA PARTY

1. Assigned

A.

Night closed as the door exposed candles
in little red jars scattered
about the room smelling of boiling tea,
a special tea of licorice and sassafras.

His hair was festooned with birds,
their songs silenced in the loose strands
weeping down the naked flesh of his back.
Birds hung at his waist
in folds and flow of Polynesian fabric,
purple of the sea, green of the mountain.
Kittens played with twine
balled and fisted on the belly of the floor.

Ship-rolled I moved into the light,
face reddened but altar-calm, took a chair
especially arranged with the only cushion,
and held the mug of enigmatic tea
terrifying in its ambivalence.
What realms would I travel from that brew?
What new worlds discover?
What birds would alight on the hair?
Would snakes peel from the mouth;
would fingers extend into lizard tails;
tongue become an angel of flight?

Tall as a priest or goddess he radiated smiles
over the late hours of the night.
He washed my feet, bathed loins,
pressed his mouth to the spirit

he thought he touched in the soul, memory.
He blew feathers on my ribs,
danced drums on my naked knees, cheekbones;
blessed prayers upon my eyelids.

The night was holy, time late.
Mystery shuddered as he knelt before me
as though asking my hands to bless his life,
confirm my secret powers.
He conjured buffaloes from my feet, armpits.
Rattles banged and shook from my teeth.
An elk reared from the floor,
floated through the glass of the dark window.
Hawks fluttered from my ears to the cracked
ceiling, a chalice trembling as wine
spilled down wretched walls of his heart splitting
in the light of those red votive candles lit
to strike the spirit of my history,
ancestry, my drums and rattles,
my curdling war cry, a bloody scalp raised
in my hands to the triumph of the night,
my face black with victory, the slain spirit
resting a pulsing liver between my teeth.
I was savior and warrior, priest and poet,
fertile and fallow, savage and prophet,
angel of death and apostle of truth.
I was the messenger of gods and demons.
He knew my powers could fathom
the darkness of the light.
I bed in Salem.

His ribs opened for my arrow;
his head split for the tomahawk, the club;
his pain longed for my hands to touch it,
soothe it, mold it into a receptacle, an urn
of blood and ashes stirred with a prayer stick

while my chants chewed the potions
that fettered his brain and soul.

I'd drink his tea and spit out rocks.
I'd suck flesh and spit out frogs.
I would paint kingfishers on his thighs,
deer on his heels, morning glories on his brow.
I would heat stones and steam off sin.
I would tear fifty pieces of flesh
to feed hummingbirds, and marry his dry bones
with Satan and they would live forever
on my fingertips, an apple bough.

Was I not touching the universe—
a feather in my hair, bells on my ankles.
Was I not master of dark dealings of dryads.
I was to raise the pipe, smoke, allow the puffs
to bathe his priesthood which he would gladly loan to me,
naming me the high priest of his foolish
pagan altar adorned with plastic geraniums and peacock
    feathers.

Pity the unanointed, the damned.
Absolve the guilty and the hangman.

B.

I switched on the bathroom light . . .
it broke the room crawling with roaches.
A canary hung dead in his greasy hair;
his flesh was caked with yellow powder;
his earlobes etched with butterfly wings.
"Turn off the light." His pain pleaded.
The candles were dipped in cats' blood.
My severed spirit had been the sacrifice.
He kissed my ring at the door
with the moon down and the cymbals silent.

C.

Boston winds pushed me into dawn,
Dogwood bloomed a street, empty and grey.
The Charles was clean, beautiful
in the morning calm. A boy
rode by on a bicycle, his blond hair
blowing free in the breeze. I was damp
with sweat and dew and could hear
the Transit grumble under my feet.
Aging bones arched, a little arthritic,
I would suppose, probably.
Potassium would help the numbing pain
and a ball to roll in the fist
would keep fingers
limp from rage and the kinks of age
in a world estranged from reality.
I picked a crocus. Its scent was fragile.
An ambulance raced past, a dog gnawed a bone.
I crossed the Charles into the grubby
Boston Common to stare at the swan boats,
consult the aging statues whitened by pigeon dung.

2.

Radio Interview

He offered me a glass of holy water
to pacify my hunger, request
for a single cup of black coffee . . .
not allowed in the sanctified confines
where only the smoke of incense curled
from the bowl of Buddha's belly.

Into the microphone he prodded voices
of black witches, magic of an alchemist,
the mystery of a grey guru lean on power

but puffed on adoration.
Gently he questioned my frozen soul.
I revealed only the colors of the day:
forsythia bloomed his April yard,
magnolias striking purple against
the Cambridge sky, the mutability
of the State, its saccharin lies.
I revealed the dirt between my toes,
lice crawling my crotch, wax building
in my ears.
Again I spoke of hunger:
a "Big Mac" would do, instant coffee,
plastic pizza, anything but holy water.

No light hung over my monk's shaped head.
No priest hid behind my coat. He smiled.
At the door he took my hand, pulled my frame
to his, whispered: "I have pain
in my throat. Can you heal the hurt?"
I offered to go home and burn sage.
I had a large can I bought once at the A&P.

Back in Brooklyn listening to the bells
of the Korean Church and the Clark St.
transistors booming out their Sunday Mass
to pigeons and shopping-bag women,
I turned on TV and watched the Marx Brothers
cavort in the old farce, "Horse Feathers."

May 6, 1980

SACRIFICE
For Joe & Carol

wolf tracks
on the snow

I follow between
tamarack and birch

cross the frozen creek
dried mulleins
with broken arms
stand in shadows

tracks move uphill
deeper into snowed conifers

I hurry to catch up
with his hunger

cedar sing in the night
of the Adirondacks
he huddles under bent
red willow
panting

I strip in the cold
wait for him to approach
he has returned
to the mountains

partridge drum
in the moonlight
under black spruce

from IS SUMMER THIS BEAR (1985)

OSHERANOHA
(Wolverine)

Under breeze
in the light
of the new moon
of the wild strawberry
into the roots
and shadows
of this clump of sumac
I give you
this old tooth
so you
will return it
straight and strong.

tekiatatenawiron

12 MOONS

Midnight. Winds tossed my wisdom-
tooth to wolverine and darkness,
sumac. It was not returned as promised,
strong and sharp.
         Again I go
with my myths to fisher. Perhaps
the moon this time in scent of river
water and wild raspberry will
be truthful. Or I shall smoke
in leaves gone dry in summer.
Akwesasne—Summer—1984

WOLF

prints in snow
scat on paths

hairs clinging to low bushes
howl on the moon

> i pull up blankets
> put the book down
> turn out the light
> and sleep again
> with your breath on my cheek

mountains move in your trot
in your smell
survive in your young
grow in the strength of your wisdom:
turtle and bear
welcome you home

RED-TAIL

Eye to eye we meet
        in my city smell
disbelief in blood
        flecked in your pupil
        my chin razor chipped
caged in the mountains
        you would take pecks of skin
        I would collect tail feathers
        you would fall to earth
        I would rise on wind
I doubt we would survive

I stared you with wonder
        wing eyed for years:
wheeling, perched, crunching bones
        on flat river-rock
You've ignored my presence
        now you must face me

deciding the poisons in my blood
deciding my heart

I have no advantage even though you are caged
        wire separated your claw
        from my liver, finger
capable of pulling the trigger

I am struck, vanquished, knowledgeable
You are too few and I too many
        you are shrew, woodchuck
        I am weed and weasel
        while you soar I thief

Eye to eye we meet
        in your meadow
        I am bee and buttercup
        fumed in strange smells
You are mole and berry seed
        you guard the east and home
        you clean the sky of vermin
        you lick the bloody stone
Where I have opened veins
        and split the bark
        wearing otter skin

RACCOON

The mountains hold my winter blood
    my shadow in its calm
The white pine, or was it tamarack,
    splintered, however, my proof
Is the silver hair embedded in the bark

Wind howled but claimed nothing . . .
    eyes closed to its ferocity

Snow, yes,
   were neither mine nor bear
But the March prints of men
   tapping maple
Circles ring the soft earth
   where pails collected heavy sap
Too cold to drink with shivering teeth

Hawk now and crow slip through sun
   hiding in the blaze
Perch fingers of beech, poplars
   eyes wading old grass, sodden
   and brown, but muscles turn
   reveal flesh to their intestines
Highways are covered with blood

Yawning into stiff but pliable dawn
   mud softening
The smells of morning:
   river and bud, plum blossom, cedar
Soil cooking its various scents
Rabbits, squirrel . . . silly chatter broke
   winter into halves
   split like a squash
Autumn nuts brought waking in the musty meat

But there was nothing
   not a box anywhere with a few crackers
   nor an open can of rotting peas
   left by the doorstep,
   or chicken bones, a dead mouse
   broomed out of the kitchen
   onto the dust pile of winter trash
The forest was bare also
   except for finch feathers
   black snow, broken nests and shells
The belly pulsed

anger choked the surprise
It stood in spring, an odd ochre
With glint of green shoots
Still bitter from snow
   not sweet under sunlight

I will study . . . muskrat, beaver
The creek was cold
   waters January teeth
   snapped into flesh, curled claw
Fishless it smelled of old willow

Determined new paths are to be scouted
   trod
   villages erected on the corpse of old
Ancient stories told in this fresh time
   as berries form, eventually,
To feed fox summer

While waiting dig for grubs, claw
   wormy wood
Expect May to be kind

BEAR

you keep the children warm

claws
      sharp they keep the woods clean
      hang from my wife's throat
eyes
      spotted elderberries and bees' wings
      kept enemies from the dark
      kept anemone in forest shade
         rats from the house

muscle/meat
  i'm sorry

       it's kept my belly
       from getting too mad at me

you've been a good friend

i'll burn these words
maybe
they'll settle over berry brambles
        smoke honey for the taste
        flavor maple sugar

you'll hear them
               these words

i'll leave suet by the big stone

Note: Wood Anemones are sometimes known as "wind flowers," as they often tremble in the breeze.

COYOTE

Over the rain I hear your howl
        toothed into night
Warming the fur, the den for pups
        your scent sealed future
While mountains melted to your print
        valleys opened to your hunger
Cows and house cats slit bellies
        for your trot into time

You survive carrying your penis in a box
        fur covered with bear excrement
        guarding your female hot with pain
        fat with preservation

Scrawny you run with hounds and poodles
        distract the gun's sight
        wearing grape leaves like a fox
When that fails you whine into legend
        creep into the house to place
        your docile paw in the lap
        your joke, story on the table

You covered the past with scat
        coffined farmers, graved moose
        managed San Diego fools
        to feed you chicken necks
        and comb your ratty tail
Your cleverness out-witted the state
        as you pointed to wolf,
        cut your own wrists
        bleeding onto lambs
        leaving gray hair
        around the bones
You are taken very seriously . . . for all the ridicule

I will bring you down and gnaw your leg
        stew your belly
        roast your shank
        hang your skull over the door
        learn and grow wise
As I consume your howl
        chew your intelligence.

WINE GRAPES

sitting in Brooklyn in the shadow of the bridge
sharp light, cold and clear, spreads
across cement and sky; fingers quiver to pick
as they did last summer sour cherry and black-cap

now autumn shadows stretch woods
a blaze on hill and meadow golden-red
frosty to the fox tongue clusters dangle
under leaves turning scarlet crunchy
to the touch reminding the pickers blueberries have finished the season currants
are drying in the shed with basil and
hickory nuts and that bear has a belly full

Wanda will jell with mint
Helen probably press for juice
Kaherawaks purple her dress
and teeth reaching into the sun
in mama's arms
for these autumnal treats

tonight with popcorn and cider
a thanksgiving for all the lovely things
of summer nourishment
earth again has provided

Larry brings a cluster to the Brooklyn
table still moistened
                    stained
by October frost and mountain chill . . .

LISTENING FOR THE ELDERS

is summer this bear
   home this tamarack
are these wild berries song
is this hill
   where my grandmother sleeps
   this river where
   my father fishes
does this winter-house

light its window for me
burn oak for my chill
does this woman sing my pain
does this drum beat
sounding waters
or does this crow caw
does this hickory nut fall
this corn ripen
this field yellow
this prayer-feather hang
this mother worry
this ghost walk
does this fire glow
this bat swoop
this night fall
does this star shine
over mountains
for this cousin who has
no aunt picking sweetgrass
for a pillow

is summer this wolf
this elm leaf
this pipe smoke
is summer this turtle
home this sumac
home this black-ash
is summer this story
is summer home
is twilight home
is summer this tongue
home this cedar
these snakes in my hair

reflection on this sky
this summer day
this bear

BROOKLYN PIGEON

Wings flash black on the sun,
trick my thinking for a quick second:

> home, winter, snow
> crow on white fields
> sun thaws iced elms
> near blue waters
> trout snagged in ice

may sun and pigeon fool my eyes
again tomorrow . . .
and sight the mountains.

GRAVEYARDS

My friend looked a little jittery.
I told Dennis that yes I could handle
the situation alone. Just get in your car
and slowly mosey on down the road . . .
no need for you to get busted.

There were the men . . . stones sitting in a row.
Little Belly, Young King, Tall Peter,
Deerfoot, Captain Pollard, Destroy Town,
Red Jacket and General Ely S. Parker.

To see their headstones under October sun
in that cemetery I remembered how Ford
and Helen took me for a drive the day before
through the mountains along the highway which
aproned the Kinzua dam to find Cornplanter's grave.
The black cat which crossed our lost
country way misled us into several wild-
goose chases. So we headed back towards Sala-

manca where I was to read poems in the new
library. Funny. We laughed pretty hard afterwards,
Helen and Robert and Ford, because we sat
in that sterling new library waiting for an audience
which hadn't been invited. One young woman,
a student, I guess, came to our table
in the children's section and expressed how much
she loved poetry and how much she would love to stay
and hear poems, but well, next time I came to
Salamanca, not then, however. Tomorrow was
a school day and she had phys-ed homework.
The four of us balled up in the yellow jalopy,
drove off to find Jerry Rothenberg's old house
in town and a Dunkin' Donuts figurin' the town
didn't want any hostile Mohawk reading poems
to their Seneca Indians. I cashed the fat check
when I got back to Buffalo . . . real fast with thanks.

Anyway, as I said, I told Dennis to get into the car,
start the motor, and leave slow. I was gonna cause
trouble. I'm really pretty proud of him, a white guy.
He did turn the ignition on, did start the motor,
but waited for my messy trouble to commence.

Right in the heart of Little Belly's stomach
stood an American flag in the traditional
"red, white and blue" . . . not synonymous
with "turtle, bear and wolf." The flag lifted
from the earth easily, and its stick broke neatly in half.

Dennis had the ol' car revved up and the door opened.
I threw down the stick, and climbed aboard.

Which reminds me. Do you know the U.S. Post Office
recently printed a 13 cent stamp to commemorate
Crazy Horse, the Lakota warrior? The proc-
lamation said because Crazy Horse had been,

and I quote, "a Great American." I think
the government is searching out his hidden grave now
to plant a small flag pole on it, too.

DEB

I celebrate your day
by singing. I count off petals
of the black-eyed susan—
one for each of your mornings,
your early sunrise,
the laughter in your afternoon.

I deck your name above
with ivy and vetch
drape columbines
around the capital "D";
entwine "E" with yarrow;
lean a single primrose against "B."

So now you have a garland
of song and flowers.
May they stay
on your lips
as spring iris always
bloom your cheek.

ARCHEOLOGIST

Out of a sandy field
of wild strawberries
he kicked up
an arrowhead,
and his foot
bled.

KAHERAWAK'S BIRTHDAY — July 28
My First Granddaughter

Crow caws against grey skies,
flies nibble the elbow as a breeze
off the summer river lifts hair
from my face waiting for sun after rain.
Letters to friends are waiting, sealed,
for posting as black-eyed susans and golden-rod
sway in down-fields bursting blooms
as dried raspberry pellets thump earth
from brambles that have completed
the labor of centuries. Noon slowly
approaches with the whistle of a train
riding the rails across the river in Canada,
disturbs the tabby cat's sleep under another
screech of crow flapping wings high
over the island. Movement by stealth movement like spider
sun at last emerges in the southern sphere.
Things splash yellow . . . even green leaves
of sumac and poplar are tainted, brushed.
Finch sings a warning to starling,
swallow zooms through the air expecting insects;
the currant is bare, the berries eaten by goats;
corn is dry but beans are heavy and onions
ready for pulling.

          This is your birthday gift . . .
this summer day and all its riches: snores
of the dog, heal-all, purple burdock,
thistle; winds and birds, weasel in the grass,
mice in the barn, berries jammed for winter, spiders,
grandma's smile, sun; turtle slipping from mud;
bear reaching into gnarled trees for honey; wolf
roaming the distant Adirondacks
and Grandmother Moon waning now in late July,
commanding her strength

to rise again tonight to bathe the dark
in colors of harvest orange which will tip
bat wings, stars and clouds drifting,
and move the river to the sea,
illuminate western wind, bring good dreams
to your sleep, happy days to your
accumulating years on this earth, years
in which you will learn to thank the sun,
Grandmother Moon, the corn and beans and squash,
the berries, herbs, the useful birds and dragon-flies,
bees, the elm and maple that reach at night
to stars that guide the hunger in the woods, light
the fisherman's path and glisten
on the scales of the fish themselves.
You will learn to thank the mysteries,
movements above and below the earth,
below the four winds, the four colors,
the four directions.
    Tonight
your father will play his guitar and sing a song
and then have a good, long smoke
while crow sleeps in its nest away from your dreams
under the lingering scent of strawberry leaves.

This is your birthday gift . . .
the old stories of the sky, waters, the earth
and winds. One day when old you, too,
will tell them on into time within the sounds
of the drum, the quiet of the mountain,
the silent flow of the river. Yes, good dreams,
good journey, many moons,
and sweet winds for your pillow.

Cornwall Island
Akwesasne 1983

HANDING THE BATON

running
    two miles
        three
running
    five miles
        ten
hawkweed leaves between the teeth
    thirst nags at both throat and feet
running into morning sun
    two miles
        three
running into sweat
    five miles
        ten
runners on the path
between
    sweetgrass and pine
runners pounding into earth
foot-prints that cannot be erased
runners running
    wolf pack
    and eagle
sun becomes eye and moon feet
noon is life-span
water eternity
running
    two miles
        three
lungs are boulders within the chest
hands relay stick to faceless hands
cool in two o'clock heat
running
    five miles
        ten
runners running breathless

      wet rags
looking for a brook to wash feet
looking for a lake to ease pain
looking for the end to breathe
looking to sky for an eagle's wing
looking north for wind

from **HUMORS AND/OR NOT SO HUMOROUS**
(1988)

APRIL 22, 1985
Spawning
For Arthur's Birthday

I hawk   the sky
wolf   the mountain
bear   the woods;

I fox   these fields
trout   this creek;

I crocus the sun
before August heat
and hungry mosquitoes
spoil this urgency . . .

ON SECOND THOUGHT

I never wanted to live in Brooklyn
with the ghosts of Crane, Wolfe and Mailer.
I never wanted to live in Brooklyn
after all your pleadings.
I hate crossing bridges
and wondering if I've crossed the right one;
or if I looked back I'd find
it consumed by the river.

I moved to Brooklyn
when you moved to Chicago;
and I've been enjoying the view
and the walk across the bridge
even if I can't spot Redhook
or hit a boat below with spit,
or catch a star.
I've never wanted to live in Brooklyn,
but I've been enjoying the ghosts
of Crane, Wolfe and Mailer.

HEARD POEM
Studio Museum Book Fair

"I used
to have
a Cherokee
boyfriend.
I knew
he was
Indian
because
he could see
a road sign
three miles
away."

GEORGE SEGAL AT THE WHITNEY MUSEUM, N.Y.C.
For Paul

It's wrong to stand
in this air-conditioned museum
spying on lovers, listening
to men talking over coffee

Their essence is individual
the silence of the soul
and the cold cold touch of plaster
static quality of motion immovable

I'm not sure these people please me
I can see them crossing the street
into nowhere grouped separately
or the exhausted penis fucked out on the bed

Do I need a taxi into this moon

light, red and blue stars washing
tired bodies, crusted minds
with souls that have only
the spirit of my spirit

Nostalgic fascination of a time
old movie marquees and rattan subway seats
into which a people are caught into art
by mistake: the art of God and Segal

I can look into my street anytime at zaftig
buttocks and smell armpits, touch frost
on coke bottles and hear gibberish:
"God it's hot." "Take a walk, brother."

The rarified is sometimes banal, too

LAST NIGHT . . .

         one
big crystal
goblet
exploded
in the middle of the floor
       on a Turkish rug

Paul and I were watching
the flick, "Gloria";
Gena
was just about to plug
a mobster
when the crystal went
b-a-n-g
we took
cover shaking
in the guts

I called Diane and Jeff
(they being crystal/spirit
expertizers)
they said shake
the house down
with burning sage
and get rid of those angers

this morning the landlady
said, nobody's been
murdered
here, but
this is Brooklyn

we slept with the lights on
in separate apts.
just in case the sage didn't work

THE COMET
Seattle, WA

In the bar
a Mohawk sings a drum
beats song into beer
bottles, coffee mugs, ears.
Coins tinkle into a hat.
While
in the men's room
atop the urinal
standing before erotic
scribbles and slogans
over the rain of piss
a vase of iris and spring
pussy-willows
embarrasses the pisser
with surprise and joy.

Macho
holding himself
with poems drumming
in the bowl
cannot compromise
with beauty.

Song enters
iris tickles spine as he turns
zips up for the next beer; rain
outside hides Mt. Rainier
but feeds sky and earth.

Confused by beauty
in such odd places
he drops his coin
amongst the tinkles in the hat.

YOUNG MALE

You sat quietly across the subway aisle . . .
raucous thunder howling in your throat,
thunder which would gag the breeze in mine.
Your tight fists are caked with sludge of cement;
hands which would slaughter six million buffalo
on the range if there were six million buffalo.
Instead, you build nuclear reactors.

Your hair is soft and loose, sports a blonde sheen;
hazel eyes send out suspicious messages,
afraid I'll scalp those flowing locks
tearing the bloody membrane from your head.
You squat on the subway seat like a mountainman
of the old as-yet-unconquered west, a green blade
ready to skin beaver or any cuss you don't much like the
crook of his jaw. Your thighs bulge, your heavy arms

are thick with electrical power of whips.
I wonder if there is a smile in your soul.
Can you bend to sniff a violet?
I doubt you'd scent anything but a double
whiskey, a hooker on the curb, your hunting boots,
your own rawness.
        Your face is not ugly
nor does it appear particularly mean, even
those hazel eyes don't seem too cruel, but when I look
at those hands knotted in a crisp clench
I know you would crush me on a whim
for you are America . . .
not the land, rivers, mountains, desert or sky,
not hawk or wolf. You are the superhighways,
skyscrapers, acid streams clogged with dead rainbows—
    and
you are Gary, Indiana; downtown L.A., Burger King,
"adult bookstores," Ronald Reagan, New Jersey
that stole the Giants and now teases the American
    Exchange.
Your prowess rumbles as the subway slides through
the harbor tunnel to Bowling Green Sta.;
when the doors open, you stand. I'm amazed to see
how short you are, shorter than me by an inch or two,
but bulky in rump and flank. We ascend the escalator;
you tramp off towards Broad St.; I amble to the Post
Office in the old Cunard Bldg. to send letters home.
I know you are here to stay
and that you are scouting buffalo.

sofky
SEMINOLE SOUP

it
takes lye,
more lye

to make it
have
good taste . . .
sweet . . .
with salt and black pepper

and boil
boil
boil

(Charley told me
in oklahoma city)

FRIENDSHIP DAYS AT AKWESASNE
Summer of '84 . . . Annual Event
For Francis

Humid afternoon by the St. Lawrence,
women canoe-racers paddle the river;
full of fry bread, soda and hot
strawberry-rhubarb pie
I stumble under the cedar arbor
to listen to the drum and singing.

Outfitted Mohawks circle a "stomp dance."
I take a place on a bench near
an elder woman who asks in Mohawk,
what do I do? Tote bag slung over my
left shoulder I figure I should own up.
"I'm a writer." . . . in smiles.
"What kind?" she asked, really curious.
"A poet," I replied proudly . . .
to which she offered a grunt,
got up from the bench and huffed off.

Well, maybe she was right.

GREYHOUNDING TO BILLINGS, MONTANA

For Shirley Sneeve Gunderson . . . who knows

"Hey! you Indian?"
I nodded.
"Hey you! You Indian?"
His cowboy hat fell onto the beercan
in his lap as he turned to his seat-companion
reading a Superman comic.
"I rode from Chi-ca-go to Minn'apolis
with these two dudes. I thought
they were greasers."
He topped his head again with the hat
and sipped his beer.
"They were reeeeal live Apaaaacheees."
I stood waiting to get into the bus bathroom.
"Hey! I asked you if you was Indian!"
Mohawk.
"From back there East?"
He sipped his beer again.
"Man, it's good sittin' next a normal person,"
and he slouched in the seat.
I agreed,
closing the bathroom door,
and turned on the bright light.

OJIBWA

Cornwall Island, Ontario

river steeped in moving storm
clouds and lightning reflected
on the sheen
        he sat on the hillock
sketching; chicory black-
eyed susans guarded the flesh
of his naked back etched by hay
stamped, tattooed with a scarlet rose

black willows bent broke
grey water rippled by eels
as afternoon shifted western wind

in the rain his skin glistened
and his long hair danced into curls
as the rose on the curve
of the shoulder-blade moistened
under patches of frail light
in which we emptied our beer cans

wet we scrambled into the truck
as the broken day bent
like the willow boughs into the water

I kissed another summer
and despaired for the rose
which would wilt on winter flesh

SEA/RIVER
After Levertov

There is a sea
        next door
just beyond Brooklyn
        I do not hear thunder
                waves
tankers splashing in the crest
fish flopping
        schools
entangled in water/weeds
        beautiful sea-flowers
thriving on brined air
        conifers and sunflowers
        white pine
rushing to shore

There is a sea
        outside
(my window has no view)
it is there, I know
        wind swells
        gulls hover
moon scales/light
        and dies
sea scent
        o scent
ruffles nostrils
my father finned
        rises in storm
o who
        is not afraid

There is a sea.
        I shall find
        the river
swim bend to pool
touching rock and curve
        each
        iris on the shore
this sea near Brooklyn
will not take
        my voice
this sea outside.
            outside.
Mountain and river
        take my flesh
in the cold bite
        of winter.

CANYON DE CHELLY
Navajo
For Jim and Terry

"You can't see unless you lean over the edge."
. . .
I leaned and floated in brittle light,
could imagine ancient Hohokam, Anasazi
going about the business of the day and dusk:
planting corn, harvesting pumpkin, chipping
arrowheads for the hunt, loving in those
dark apartments, women toting clay jars of water . . .
squirrels, mice cacheing for winter. A crow
broke the fantasy and I remembered Simon
telling his son not to forget the Navajo blood,
"wolves of the mountains," shed by Kit Carson
in 1864. My spine was pinched with chill.
The groans of the dying were in the caw of crow,
in wind; blood smelled from canyon walls.

We drove from one lookout to another: Antelope
House, Standing Cow, Mummy Cave, Massacre Cave.
Simon's poem persisted in my ear.

We drove Jim's Fiat across the windy reservation
to Chinle and ate good fry bread and hot chili
in a plastic diner owned by a Navajo family.
. . .
Now I'm in New York's canyons searching
for Simon's old poem.

1/28/81
FIFI

One

I will say simply you were a woman
who gave me two hawk feathers
your grandfather respected.
They hang on a twig from the woods
which berths a sparrow nest in my study.
I see them each day. The cat teases them.
I often say I shall write.
Once a month or so I find your address.

You claimed something special for these feathers.
I asked if they'd keep harm away;
would they fulfill dreams;
revive an old persistent love.
Your laughter brushed off the desert morning . . .
"You'll see," you replied, the sun on your lips.

Two

Today as I was looking at the feathers
and promising a note the mail arrived from Gallup.
Jim wrote you'd been in town,
that your truck was hit by a semi
on your road home to Hopi.
You had been killed.

As I mull over feathers and notes and death
Sula sits in my lap seeking attention.
It's snowing here in Brooklyn.
I need to write letters.
The cat nibbles my pen.

GHOST DANCE
For James Walsh

You know Wovoka was a poor tailor
and could not sew shirts
to withstand the teeth of the wind.
The dance is the dancer.

Sitting Bull is buried,
but his children bore children.
We must bite the flesh where it hurts,
and let sage burn in Brooklyn and Oakland.

We hunt together;
rats chatter in the tunnels of our bones;
children suck on canned poisons.
But you know all this.

You know the children must not stumble . . .
though doctors may reset bones
and heal blistered burns.
Our mother was murdered.

Alcatraz is no mythical island . . .
knees bend to old stories.

MUSSELING
La Jolla

tide out
wet skirt licks brown thighs
caught in Pacific light
drifting into your dawn
striking the blood
cuts of fingers knived, salted
on black shells not
willing to budge from rocks.

Wanda, the baby cries,
wine sours in the jug;
your hair runs flecks of grey . . .
scented of basil.
there is still wilderness
in your hike up Torrey Crest,
smell of pine,
poppies at your waist;

there are miracles in your hands
as you lope the beach
collecting sea-shells, gull-down;
crawl meadows for sorrel,
arrange dried yarrow.
can't subtract words
to your daily verve
nor epithet your verb.

tide in, tide in
covers mussels to rock.

noon demands attention.

OROVILLE HIGH, CALIFORNIA

I can't believe I'm eating a cheeseburg
in Oroville, CA, where dogs yelp at ghosts.
What I can't really believe is eating
the cheeseburg in a classroom at Oroville High
among students taught the mastery of printing.
They're ambivalent to instruction,
indifferent to machines which will record
their births and local football games . . .
machines which are indifferent to Oroville
itself, the buttes beyond the town's
rigid limits where Ishi clawed rock desperately

struggling to preserve his unrecorded songs;
a school where no student knows nor cares
about the almond groves nor the gold
that built Oroville, let alone
Ishi's drum, nor the crisis of extermination,
not even their own.

INUIT

> *"I wish I kill myself like hell."*
> —Inuit teen-ager, as reported
> in the *New York Times,* 11/10/79

I write this on barroom walls.
It spells the death of caribou.
I forget we are the eaters of raw meat.

The northern moon freezes on my cheek.
There must be some bird in imitate;
I forget the words of the morning songs.
I will put my ear to the ice . . .
it remembers.

LISTENING TO LESLIE SILKO TELLING STORIES, NYC 2/8/79

I take February ice and chill
in stride, enter the subway
to write the various faces
sitting to either side
know children will always listen
as the train shuttles from magic
to Brooklyn

from **GREYHOUNDING THIS AMERICA** (1988)

I WATCHED RAVEN TAKE THE SKY

We drove out to the Shinnicock
powwow, drank beer,
ate sugared fry bread,
prowled around the rezz . . .

She took it all in . . .
feathers and drums,
English prayers
and teenaged dancers
painted and plumed.

On the way back . . .
snug in her Volks bug
and, I guess, safe-feeling
with a cold coke
and almost home again . . .
she leaned over a little
my way and said:

"How come
you don't
have an
Indian name?"

I watched the raven take the sky.

A PARTIAL EXPLANATION
Thoughts of John Berryman

All month the moon has been reaching
for the pear tree. Now the black fruit
and leaves move in wind off the marsh.
A fox yips across the wide meadow;
raspberries and the sea scent the air.

Conversation is slow, stilted . . .
words hard as the August pears, color
of the leaves . . . though the moon
threads its light over quiet faces.
The house dog groans in the dark

neither scenting basil in the dooryard
nor aware of the fox's pain under the stars.
The moon moves through the sour apple
and drops among juniper and oak.
"Ciao!" The apt response . . . "Ciao."

MARCH RESERVE:
Long Island
Apology to R. E.
For Helen Rundell

Light struck your cold hand;
a woodcock eyed your camera . . .
not twinge nor twitch when the trigger clicked;
skunk cabbage coursed through March sludge;
crocus winked at the morning sun;
two herd of deer on either side of the wood
nibbled new shoots, and like cows
stared us down the path until the light
took our footsteps into brown mirage.

What happened, Helen, to the wilderness . . .
we found chicken feathers
opossums left scattered among the rocks.

Cedars whistled in the wind;
pine cones popped; rusty oak tinkled
Japanese glass; afternoon
slithered over moss and green lichen;
light stopped on the hollow of a log;

the eddy of the Connetquat, in the bent
dry grass winter forgot to mow and hung at the edge . . .
wild hair of the witch of the forest.

Light and color and shade are absolved;
not the wilderness in men.

If we have twenty years to tramp these woods . . .
deer will take salt from your hand,
fox will suck grapes in your lap,
ospreys will place beaks to our lips;
light will be stone, and narcissus
cleared
from the mirror of the treacherous pool,
in the gold intellectual light the bones
of the groundhog will have been devoured,
the forest floor escalated into highways!

What is happening, Helen, to the wilderness . . .
dry winds on gloved hands!

Yet, summer will push deer to seek
dark leaves of the hickory woods,
crocus and squirrels may pass, black
elderberrys will dangle in the sun,
and watercress bed in sluggish streams.
Perhaps this fence about this wild reserve
is not as foolish as it seems, Helen.

DOGWOODS

pale petals
litter
Newark
avenues . . .
the only

touch
of spring
in the Jersey
junkyards
of McDonalds
and broken faces
bitter
closed
to May time

CYCLIST

movement through moist morning
met jimson in the valley of death
and tripped on wheels
into motion of mooned midnight

mysterious seas swell
in the groin and stomach
as he crashed
into the vermilion sunset
of crazy joy

wind between the teeth
sky woven into hair
clouds on the shoulders
sun biting cheeks;
the whole earth rounding
the curve of the wounded road

midnight found a nest of stars
imprinted on his helmet
whirring in his particular sphere
and he thought of the prisoners
in their enclosed, expensive cars

FOR CHEROKEE MARIE
Who May Have Forgotten

earth strong in the blood
fleas cannot suck from veins
blood rich in the sun

mountains explode on the chest
of western plains, birds scale
clouds over broken graves

torn by wolves and puppies
blood feeds berries, the white bones
of Crazy Horse were never found

the lance flowers the earth
blood thickens as braided hair
the spider spins in the sun

SAND CREEK, COLORADO
100 Years After

Night thick as heavy voices
or the plod of cattle rattling
in the farmer's garbage dump

coyotes called ancient shadows
Cheyenne whose fires burn low along the creek
to light the collection of the dead
bones wolves chose not to chew

the state marker says nothing
of the women, the children
or White Antelope's cry . . .
"nothing lasts but grass and mountains . . ."
choked by the butt of his penis
soldiers thought a joke

wandering in sacred screams
holy terror and extermination
picking the snot of gold from Chivington's nose
he stuffed to the stench of his kill

thin hands found our faces
our dog whined and hid beneath the Datsun
hungry mouths of children
sought her breasts and would have sucked
had she opened her blouse

sleep was safe in New York
exhausted in the numb and nulled morning
we counted cigarette packages, beer cans
orange peels and civilization
and left the dead to comfort the dying
while in the dark birds sing

history's blood has grown its spring crop of grass
tall cottonwoods stand central to the scholar
lofty rock peak dawn to citron morning

MONAHSETAH
. . . A Cheyenne Girl
For the Hochs of Denver

Evicted into the frozen teeth of winter
by the landlords of the plains;
Cast into the bloody waters of the Washita
Where your father's corpse flowed in the stream . . .
His manhood stuffed into his mouth,
His scalp made guidon for Custer's soldiers.
Torn from the band of helpless captive women,
Your suckling child, mewing and puking in your arms;
Driven by Long Hair to feel out the ashes of the village,
Scout out the vital hearts of your people.

Did Sheridan's hands fondle the sweetness
Of your young Cheyenne nipples;
Did Custer mount you like a stud until
His civil wife pulled his sweaty thighs
Off from the Cheyenne Mystery of your life!
You held your childish hands to your womb
And felt the kickings of a bird, the fledgling sperm
Planted like so much corn by yellow-locked Long Hair!
Where did you find the love to mount his cot, knifeless,
Or did he find your flesh upon his earthen floor!

Custer strutted your grave to glory, foolish girl!
Now in the winds of the Washita Valley cottonwoods cry
For the slain Cheyenne. No wind moans in the leaves
For the head-strong girl, daughter of Little Rock,
Who followed the tails of the pony soldiers.

SACAJAWEA

(who led the Lewis and Clark expedition to the Rocky Mountains,
and was consequently reunited with her people, the Shoshones,
having been held a captive of the Mandans for many years)

We had traveled far to that winter which crouched
On the land like the paw of a cougar
Sucking the warm blood of an antelope.
We had traveled far into that future.
In our buffalo robes we had brought the first Christmas
To the frozen mountains, and to my people
Who stood off from the joy, the festivities
And the brandy, who stood awed in the darkness
By the medicine of my two white chiefs.
The Shoshones had not recognized my braids.
But as I modestly spoke Lemhi, my sister stepped
Out to claim my blood from the distant past.

And then my people gathered and stared at Cruzatte
And Gibson who with frost-bitten fingers plucked fiddles,

And watched through the naked trees these strange men
Dancing to the horn and the tambourine.
Venison turned on the fire and the grease
Drippings spattered on the hot stones and coffee brewed
While my son suckled and bit my breasts.
I felt the fresh spirit of an unknown god
Creep into my being and itch the heel of my foot
To dance out a joy and a pleasure I had not felt
Ever before in my young life as a child with my people
The Shoshones, or as a slave of the fierce Mandans.

My French husband, rough and drunk on whiskey
Hung glass beads on the junipers, and that night
Took me into his blanket without beating me first.
Peering out from the furs, I saw snow sparkle downward,
Hitting and sizzling on the fire which had been kept burning
To hold off the wolves. I smelled Charbonneau, his flesh
And his breath; felt his hands poking my breasts,
Fumbling across my thighs, my thoughts.
I was pleased but not because of my husband's attention,
Nor the story Captain Red Clark had told of the Jesus . . .
I was at peace with myself:
I was once more amongst my people,
And my body lay warm and quiet upon my earth.

FRAGMENT

The wolf
has no tears
for the aged
rabbit
in its jaw!

THE YELLOWSTONE

I

The cat paws of dawn scratch
the edges of the Yellowstone
while overhead the sky fills with brightness
and under orange cottonwoods startle
the eastern eye, worry the deer.
The morning whistles flushed out rabbits
and three pheasants frightened into flight.
The Yellowstone has been turning since creation,
and dawn has been falling down mountains
to drift into coulees before the first arrow was shaped.

II

The conductor punched tickets in Butte, Montana;
gold trickled out of the Rockies, out of Shoshone blood!

III

This river knows no other course . . .
nor does the Ohio nor the Missouri;
the Yellowstone has shared its waters and beavers
with all explorers, slaked the Crow's thirst
and Red Cloud and even Custer.

The river moves on.
The train doesn't lose sight of the shoreline
and the mallards and geese and stark willows
and the antelope paths leading into canyons;
and ghosts fishing its pools
and the dark and sacred mountains rising.

The explorer stops to hunt,
the hunter to war,
the warrior to occupy,
the occupier to ranch.
This river moves on.

Geese fly north to Canada.

IV
When the summer sun his hottest the river
will shrivel . . . wait for winter snow;
it will narrow under wild plum trees;
it will fatten with the inevitable April floods.
The river moves on
slowly across the land, stark and dusty,
red with the blood of Crazy Horse,
silent to the echoes of shrapnel and the thud
of falling flesh; the waters move
though raccoons come to drink
and trout hide in secluded pools.

V
James Welch drinks a beer
in Missoula,
and writes his poems.

VI
The Yellowstone creates no music, no noise . . .
even the rapids' whisper is deadened
by the glass pane of the passing window;
it feeds the locoweed and the magpie
and the children of Sacajawea.
It collects no taxes and builds no temples.
It takes nothing along with it
but perhaps a fallen Chinaberry or hereford
or the broken wing feather of an eagle.
This river moves on.
It pushes a little mud,
leaves a little silt,
sucks a little sun.
The Yellowstone changes its course slowly,
it forgets the empire,
it leaves an islet in the stream;

uncovers rock, bones of old ones;
possibly a rusty musket of Colter or Bridger,
or the bleached jaw of an elk
caught in the bite of a winter blizzard.

VII
Buffalo thundered the shores,
children bathed in its waters,
Black Elk prayed to its spirit.

VIII
The Yellowstone contracts and purples to dusk;
evening stars rumple upon an eddy;
the moon rises over ripples;
mosquitoes spurt from the shoreline;
ravens roost cottonwoods;
an owl whispers; coyote sniff mice.

The train moves into Idaho at night
through the mountain country of Montana,
the home of the Crow and Cheyenne,
We drift into a conclave of stars.
The river moves on
under the smoke of the train within
the time of an eye, and a drum; within
the time of a rifle and plow
and the hoof of sheep rutting the grasses
with teeth which have nibbled the hills bare.

IX
Ghosts wail by campfires
under those Yellowstone stars.
Black Elk prayed.
A rabbit fears its skin, its flesh
as the hunter steps through the brush.
A goose honks in the darkness.
The Yellowstone follows its course.
Deer come to drink!

The train blows the whistle in the night
over the flow of the river.
I close my notebook for sleep,
remembering that Reno was probably drunk
and Custer ambitious.

X
In the morning a hawk will take the skies!

MONET
Tsalie, Arizona

blue sage purpled
within the red desert

caught in the crow's shadow
seeking higher clouds

where your brush and my pen
may not scale these colors

light drips off fingertips
into pools of image

sage, pinion-blue, blue
against blue, and time tips

petals; heat waves
rise from this bunch of sage

blue in the dawn
scarlet in the sun.

light peels like bark
on junipers, my hands remain empty.

WHEN IN REALITY

I wrote in my journal
I had eaten only an orange
and some cheese this morning.
and drunk a pot of coffee dry.
When in truth, at dawn, I had eaten
lizards, coyotes, silver and cactus
and a lone laborer in the desert.
I drank sky, sun and clouds;
my eyes consumed plains, mountains,
countries, continents;
worlds rumbled in my belly.
Tonight I slice and fork the western moon,
crunch on stars
and drink the whine of wolves.

CANYON DE CHELLY, RETURN—1978
For Jim Ruppert

I
From the rim noon and the crow
are the very same. Imagination
cannot break those ancient ruins.

II
Enter from Chinle, the floor absorbs;
knowledge clatters like cottonwood leaves
turning August gold: moon sketched on walls
where turkeys run. We have not perceived
the rhythm of the drum, nor our eyes
identified the dancers' steps, nor worn
antelope skins about the loins.

III
Marauding Spaniards, or Kit Carson's

thieving recruits . . . we enter seeking
ripe peaches and the touch of crumbled walls.

Three crows fly darkening skies;
Willie Mustache tells old stories,
old horrors of search and destroy,
that Anasazi youths once scaled
those unscaleable cliffs before Coca
Cola invented rheumatism.

IV
Our presence has shifted light;
cigarette stubs, the lead gasoline fumes
are hammers against adobe dust.
We have gawked at the flesh,
and contorted, tattooed shadows.

V
Exit. Supper in Chinle:
hamburgers, ice tea. We have moved
with clouds, the blue bunting
which followed our truck, but have not
left a peach stone to gather time.
We go home to watch movies on tv
and calculate diplomas and salaries.

VI
Lookouts on the rim designate
the past, lean into time. From the rim
we can revere both the star and the crow,
and those people who defied destiny
by clinging to walls with tooth and nail,
absorbed in the task of surviving brutal winds.

NOVEMBER SIERRAS, 1976

For Peter

Moon partially eaten
by hungry coyotes
yapping on the hills for mice.
Sugar pine cones drop in the dark
of the raccoon forest;
firefly stars hang in manzanita brush;
two men on stumps huddled
over mugs of steaming cedar tea;
huddled over words on frosty air;
shivering, we heard coyote sing,
and talked of home north
in the Adirondacks
sitting on the ridge
in that brittle light.
The moon shifted tall ponderosas.

Mohawks in Paiute country;
and speechless Louis arguing
with phantoms of the November sleep!
Rosebud tracking moles!

Our words touched
as the mugs
and our poems!
We pissed and entered
the cabin . . . you to Sarah,
and my hypered exhaustion
to the moonlit bunk
near the wood stove.

There is no message, Peter,
but the yapping of the dogs
and the falling of the moon
and the freeze on the dawn.

WANDA ON THE SEASHORE
Pacifica

You glean the sea, you and your beachcomber
With the fiery beard and the glinting eye;
You are the sea, you and your friend,
Dunking-in-the-raw of the red light of the sun
On into the smile of the moon, taking a beer, coffee;
Cooking the fish you caught;
Gathering shells . . . the weird wind in your hair . . . ;
Clamming with your big toes in the sand and mud;
Hunting ghost crabs, scraping mussels;
Your hut . . . broken, airy . . . leans as the wind leans
Through domes of dune above the shore in range
Of storms. You have a hell of a time,
You and your beachcomber and the mongrel dog:
You steal off and find a field of painted-Indian-brush
Somewhere along the road, your skirt swollen,
Falling around your legs and thighs,
Your fingers stained from Wild blackberries.
You are living the sea, dining on grass,
Fingering the dark greenness of the woods.
I am grey in this great grey city!

BASHO'S POND

Willows guard
The frog's bath;
Gaiety is splashed about.
Why are the waters dark!

Basho has slept
Three full cycles through
Within this twilight ritual
His serenity broods.

The effect
Of calm; the willows tear
The water's glaze . . .
The curtains part.

A scratch of sundown,
Vermilion, breaks the trees
Upon the pond.

READING POEMS IN PUBLIC

I stand on a stage and read poems,
poems of boys broken on the road;
the audience tosses questions.

I tell of old chiefs swindled of their daughters,
young braves robbed of painted shields,
Medicine Man hitting the bottle;
I chant old songs in their language
of the Spirit in wind and water . . .
they ask if Indians shave.

I recite old stories,
calendar epics of victory battles,
and cavalry dawn massacres on wintered plains,
villages where war ponies are tethered to snow . . .
and they want to know
how many Indians commit suicide.

I read into the microphone,
I read into the camera,
I read into the printed page,
I read into the ear . . .
and they say what a pretty ring you wear.
The tape winds, the camera reels,
the newspaper spins

and the headlines read:
Ruffian, the race horse, dies in surgery.

At the end of the reading they thank me;
go for hamburgers at McDonalds
and pick up a six-pack to suck
as they watch the death
of Geronimo on the late show.

I stand on a stage and read poems,
and read poems, and read . . .

from **THE SHORT AND THE LONG OF IT** (1990)

IN THE VINES

For Oakley in Wisconsin
At Oneida Nation

voices /
he heard voices
painted on the belly of the bridge
over Duck Creek
he knew they were a people /
nation

voices talking of the vines
of wild strawberries
crawling along the creek edge
of the white/pink trilliums
spattering the wood's floor . . .
snows of spring

a voice urging him to tramp
the ferns and mosquitos of the woods
looking for dinosaur eggs
large as Olmec head sculptures

he knew their haunts /
voices/writings
and we sat below the bridge listening /
listening
and all I heard were the scrawls . . .
"I love Kim" and "B.I.A. go home"

he asked what they said
he knew they were a people/nation
stranger amongst strangers
perhaps lost/hungry/wounded

how could I explain . . .
his hands were so fragile

how could I tell him who they were . . .
he was a spring blossom himself
how could I bring heart-break
to his fantasy/his boy smile
his six years as he sat anxious
believing and listening
as the berry vines curled
around his ankles and wrists

CITATION
At St. Lawrence University
(Thinking of Al Glover)

burial
old ghosts
whining from the past
hands reaching out
to greet
cautious smiles
remembering, often,
terrible things
boy-hood pain growing
reticence
blood on the lip and heart
black night on the jaw

my father standing there
grinning
a tooth missing in front
his tongue trying to cover up the gap
hands deep in his trouser pockets
later,
no, earlier,
Mama leading his Chevy
through winter and blizzard
gripping a kerosene lantern

to show the dead road
(my father gripping the wheel)
home to grandma's coffin

whiteness of day
pall on the brilliant shine
sun touching Louie's cheek
Al's chin
university chapel ringing bells
as black robed professors
priest-chant across the green

there stood Stewart and Alex
Angus' aura
river moving
boats chopping cold waters

dream me back to ghost arms
dream me back to open fields
autumn smoke lifting off bare branches
dream me back to hickory nuts
bare-back riding the blind horse
gathered in childhood hands
Aunt Ruth laughing at our giggles
dream me back, dream me back
into ghost arms

Mama angry in blizzard and storm
winter as cold as these new-born ghosts

PRAYER FOR PHILIP DEERE
In The Sierras

four directions
four winds
        we sat

huddled near corn-grinding holes
four heads
      bowed below the sun
      in prayer
sun burnt faces browned
winds blew loose hair
to the four directions
in the four winds
      sun was there
      moon
      stars waited for darkness
      waters shimmered blue in the lake
      the great granite rock held
        four figures

to the east
to the south
to the west
to the north
      winds blew
      yellow, red, blue, black
green mountains towered behind us
bluejays danced
ground squirrels and swift black lizards
darted in and out of holes in the earth
in the distance children were playing
a rowboat plied the metallic waters
  (two women sat drinking beer on the path)

to the east
      she spread the red blanket
to the south
      she drew out the pipe
to the west
      she gave the pipe tobacco
to the north
      she lit and raised the pipe

                    passed
                    again, and once more
                    passed once more again
to the winds, waters, sun and the moon
to stars, clouds, night and to day
to fish, birds, deer hiding in brush
to laughter of the children
(to the two women squatting on the path)
to blackberry bush ripening in blossom
to the great oak fastened to golden hills
to earth tightly gripped in the fist
to Mother Earth
four burnt faces, burnt brown by sun
brown by blood of ancestry
four winds
which had long ago
scooped out
corn-grinding holes in the rock
leaving them to cup sun or rain,
for pounding acorn or green corn
    fresh from harvested fields

she raised the pipe
        bluejay sang
she raised the pipe
        lizard flicked his tail
she raised the pipe
        to the winds
four bowed heads burning brown
        beneath the sun
jimson opened to flower
bees gathered
verbena stretched to the lake
birds gathered clouds passed overhead
sun passed through
lake water sparkled
fish swam free

she raised the pipe
> prayers ascended into the sky
> in all directions
> to four winds
> east, south, west, north
> to sun, moon, water, earth
she raised the pipe
> silence
fell upon the afternoon
bluejay ceased singing
lizard held tight his raised tail
ground squirrel's eyes peeped across the entrance
oak did not waver in the stilled breeze
light fallen upon the lake water
mirrored the great flow of rock
as sun watched moon rise in the sky

green mountains stood in beauty
> > quiet
datura closed petals
silver hard on the lake water
magpie stopped chattering
as hawk wheeled across the endless sky
shot with the burst of scarlet sunset
as thunder rolled
> in the far, far
> > distance

POSTCARD

Framed
> (Currier & Ives)
> it stands the rigors
of winter
dressed in jackets of snow
settled within the bosom

of the mountains
at the side of a lake

pine aroma
        aging flesh
and aging buildings
one blue and balconied
historic on the hill-side street
        (for sale)
caught my eye
        and pause
and I'd coffee at Alice's Restaurant
where I could see the blue
building better
and smell bear and fox
not far beyond
in the mountain wood
in green winter woods
carved out by wind and snow
green as any dream

but the postcard
with many greetings
the emergency hoot
at all hours
sounding fog
(or ship horns of fog)
far from any sea
and the ancient
J. J. Newberry Co.
                the only one
left in the world
probably
dressed holiday
sold funny things
you can't buy in big cities,
or Yum Yum Tree

with chocolate truffles
              windowed
filling the street
with o those smells
sweet and tempting and fattening
with Mary's smile and Peg's
candy tease
and the ladies come for tea
to peck at gossip
Norine to smoke
Cathy to coffee
get a look at me
pony-tailed stranger
in a strange country

postcards
I mailed off
          hundreds
to friends and family
              of bears
at Onchiota
              and hawks
              lakes
and burning mountains
leaves like lemon-drops
and limes and dollops of blood
(Dierdre said)
                  licked
hundreds of 14 cent stamps
as now I mail off this card

but you can't know
              Yum Yum
              nor Dewdrop
              nor Pendragon
              nor the Java Jive
until you've seen them framed

in their setting,
or the
   "good morning, stranger"
as you pay for the *Times*
to get the world news
which you don't need
     anymore
you have become a figure
in the tourist postcard
see, see
   there you are!
leaning against the old hotel
see, see
   the one in blue wool hat
and the blue tennis shoes
you have melted
    like wax
blown into the scene
     blown glass
from the artist's flute
       yes,
"nice to see you"
nice to see that you are
a minute color beneath the gloss
yes, that's you, you
the lady is speaking to you
"have a nice day"
"I'm so happy to see
you in the paper"
Ms. Dudley was wont to say

a line drawn into
    the scene
framed in holiday, festival
      and snow
can't you hear bells ringing
the old man standing

before the downtown library
why, he's ringing bells
bells, bells, bells
before the empty lot
where the movie house was destroyed in fire
(and now rebuilt)

and snow
falls on his bells
and the ringing ceases
muffled
is carried off by the winds
or the night descending
thick and dark
on the village
moving slowly onto the lights
as if some great animal
an enormous bear, perhaps
moved out from the winter woods
to enfold you
in dreams
(a dog barks in the town hills
a taxi moves through swirls
of wind
a lone student ambles down the street
muffler tossed about the throat
its redness brightening the sky
towards laughter throbbing Main Street
the fog horn and a babe wail . . .
"nice to see you"
the dog barks once more)

in dreams
is that what it was
a dream, nothing
more than a dream
interlude

(tamarack, cedar, hemlock
dipped in chocolate
                    a truffle)
flute notes of wind
blowing through birch boughs
and cedar
        cedar sing over my mother's grave
will it sing to me
over mine
        stranger stalking
        then, now, forever, maybe
the village streets
                    winter wind and snow
aroma of pine and bear
chilled to the bone
will cedar sing over mine

as I drop this in the post box
I'm in hopes you will
receive it by Thursday

P.S.
I forgot
to mention
Robert Louis Stevenson
wrote fiction
                (and poems)
here

A VILLAGE IN THE HIGH PEAKS OF THE
    ADIRONDACKS

WINTER'S END

mush

WALKING WOODS WITH DOGS
After a Snow Fall

A green pristine only a miracle could devise
green color of lake water
billowed in foam
     foam of snow
And, odd, high on a naked tamarack
a banana peel dangles in forest light
some bird will supper

English setters pounce through the banks
noses rutting the fluff
          tails snapping
against a sapling birch
         barks echoing

Spruce sags and white pine under snow
         your
shoulders deep in mystery of thought
end of the year soon to replace holiday

You cannot see the mountains . . . Marcy or Whiteface
through the green needles, yet they are collecting
winter on shoulders, too
You cannot hear loons
     lakes and ponds frozen to flight
Yet they are there with bear snoring into spring
raccoon plotting the dangling banana peel
deer quietly waiting the setters
        leave
and the crunch of your heavy boots
skunks trailing the scent of dog meat on your hands

Have you dropped bread on the snow for swallows
        or
your own return

Setters, too, can lose the way in blizzards
as snow covers track and scent while conifers bend
disfiguring the scene you remember these years
of challenging wood and mountain

You have known your way
            always through winter
whatever corridor you stalked
but now in the broad light of this green afternoon
among these green trees, snow covering thin creeks
which yapped like puppies in summer, covering
the dead housecat fox took down months ago
                    there
there, hear it, do you hear it?
the howl? is it wind in the trees, pine
or some spirit of the woods attempting
            seeking
or, is it merely wolf searching its den and young
You shake your head in total disbelief
shake snow off your shoulders
stomp your boots, whistle for the dogs
                    time
time to go home in the green light
as it darkens on your face
            green
wind bites your green cheek and smile as you stop
listen to the silence now that the dogs
                    stand
erect tails to the wind as if frozen in frost

You look up
    the banana skin still hangs too high
for raccoon
    a bluejay wings off knocking
snow puffs to a fallen log crumbling in age
you must go back to the house
wood to chop for the stove, reports to make

your wife has a plate of cold chicken for a snack
and wild grape jam for a slice of hot toast
                coffee
so black it will stand your hair on end
You start the return
        think a moment before calling
the dogs, your stance perfectly still
and realize the setters have already reached the backyard
You listen
   the howling has faded into the approaching
                        gloom
pause to catch the scratching of raccoon on bark
fox crunching bones of a bird
or the late flight of summer mallards

Smiles break open
        you drop a glove on the purple snow
sniff, rub the back of your hand against your cold nose
and know there is time
again tomorrow you will walk woods
                with dogs
touch snowflakes with a warm tongue
                listen
fall of light and the hush of darkness
swallowing these green woods
                green
as new spring fermenting in the earth

TAMARACK

It was a house
a real house
with kitchen and beds,
living-room and bath

It wasn't really a tree

and yet it was made
of raw wood
smelling a forest
green and ripely logged

It wasn't really a tree
though odd birds lived there . . .
cats and poets,
basketball players,
a guitarist whose music twang
was never heard,
bear hunters
who couldn't shoot straight nor home game

It was a tamarack
but it wasn't a tree
it wasn't a tree . . .
I'm quite sure
it wasn't a tree

ON THE SUN PORCH — PRE-DAWN
For Joe

First heavy clouds.
Dispersed.
Wind rushes the hill,
strikes brick and glass;
rattles panes of sight.

Snow enters the noise.
First, falls slovenly.
Whirls of white flames
dash against glass
as if it would slap the cheek
exposed above blankets
sliding off the cot bed.

Suddenly ears are assaulted
by the storm heaving
against survival
of weak senses.
All passions of nature
explode. Ears panic.

Push through the imaginary
and the real
of first drawn when light
is so frail.

Ah! mountain move
Allow the sun this morning.
Or day . . . retreat.

ROBERT LOUIS STEVENSON COTTAGE
Saranac Lake, N.Y.

"I've had enough
writers here,"
the owner said.
"They can tear up
your mind,"
he cautioned
when I inquired
for summer occupancy.

He closed
the conversation
and so I moved into
a house
of chocolate truffles,
instead.

MYSTERIES

For Tehanetorens

I

I watched him take down the chicken-wire fence.
His white mane brighter than sun,
His face blue/twilight chicory
as the morning light careened above spruce and pine.
He carried lightness and yet his shoulders drooped;
His hands empty except for a hammer
to pull the mesh away from the garage walls.
He stepped about holding mountains in his hands.

II

There was nothing left on the shadowed floor
but shadows and a single feather.
Neither a smear or speck of blood
showed either death or war.
He had cleaned the mess;
brown feathers scattered here and there,
two stuck in the mesh of the wire;
one embedded in the cement wall.
He washed away the blood
except for a stain on his own chin.

III

His account was brief.
There was no need to garnish that event.
"I came out yesterday morning as the sun
struck the tops of that white pine
traveling east to southward
with a handful of corn.
He'd been a friend . . . two years.
Two years past we met on the forest floor—

he, drowsy from pain of a broken wing.
Two years I fetched feed and water.
Felt the wing grow in strength,
told him stories and listened as he told stories
to me . . . his flights across the skies,
the mountain trees, his hours waiting prey
on a lone and naked bough of an elm long dead,
of flights into sky, distant sky of airs and lands
we can't know ourselves. He'd speak
of many mysteries men might need to know
but find them difficult to understand.

"I came out here this morning
glad to know sun would shine today
and no rain fall. A tanager whistled
on that new wood fence across the road
and chipmunks squeaked in the low branches
of these cedars. I think I whistled with the bird.
It was a new day. I'd passed the darkness
of the night once again. A hot cup of coffee
in my hand: my wife put a good breakfast on her table.
I was thinking Jesus had been a real man, and good.
The garage door was open a crack.
Blood smeared the jamb low down
close to the ground. I threw the door open.
The floor was littered with feathers.
A hole torn in the mesh; more blood on the cage floor.
I knew his spirit was in flight
to those mysteries I spoke before. I knew
this raccoon . . . well, it's natural.

IV

"Tooth and claw," the Christian Bible says.
Somehow I'd suppose it's probably right.
I won't hate the raccoon nor cherish my bird
the less. He struggled to live. More my fault than his.

I put him to death; I signed the paper and paid
the claw and tooth to execute.
What makes me feel bad is that we didn't have
a chance to have a last chat."

V

Lightness in his hands he carried mountains.
Sun on his mane, his face was dark.
He rolled the wire and dragged it outside
as though it were a heavy stone.
He stacked the 2×4's that formed the cage,
saying they'd make a good fire.
He looked up into the sky.
"I'm mean today. Gotta lot of work to do."

DUG-OUT
A Mohawk Speaks to a Salvaged Past

> *In 1984, when workers drained out of the ponds at a private estate near Malone, N.Y., to repair a dam, two dug-out canoes were discovered preserved in the mud. Before they were excavated, leaders at the nearby Akswesasne Reservation were contacted and invited to be present. It is rare for wooden artifacts to survive long in such excellent condition, and carbon dating has revealed them to be between 400 and 500 years old. Though it has not yet been firmly established which of the Indian peoples then using the region may have built them, the find has distinct archaeological significance for anyone living in the North Country, and especially for the Mohawks of Akwesasne.*
>   *The poet Maurice Kenny was one of the Mohawks present at the excavation. The poem that follows grew out of the discovery and the feelings it engendered in Kenny and other members of the Akwesasne community. Kenny . . . has called "Dug-Out" one of his most important works.*
>   *—Chris Shaw (copyright 1987 by Chris Shaw /* Adirondack Life)

DUG-OUT

Ancient hollowed canoe discovered in the mud bottoms of Twin Ponds near Malone, New York, in the summer of 1984 — For Salli and Lloyd.

rainbows clean the sky
end in the leaves of a pitcher
which collects bows and rain
and the plants' bloody flowers
trumpet the morning and storm finishes
clearing the sky, the forest floor
the pond etched by fern and pine

holding a chip of wood no thicker than a fat sliver
pond water slurping against tiered banks
and floating logs under the slow flight of coots
July broke crows' raucous warning woods opened
to swamp rose, to tamarack, black willow and oak
a rough path through brambles, eryngo, blue flag
and arrowhead; earth wet, bog, rich and dark mystery
. . . a mere sliver, fat but crumbly in fingers
capable of picking pitcher plant
to heal burnings in the chest . . . the common cold

     silver water ripples decades pass to shore

     not really but sounds of stone hammers
     pounding thick log drums woods, echo down time
     quivering in this silver, this sliver, now

     voice: frightening intonation, warning as crow cawed

what is this hair embedded in the gray grain
of this wood/shingle
perhaps hundreds of years
near 19 feet long, 2 feet wide

     egret tells time in the flap of a wing
     sweaty labor digging

brown feather floats down from over-head branches
rests upon water turning golden
in this our afternoon, this summer day
eons away, an afternoon which can't hear
egrets or the fall of feathers tipped black
for victory or death . . . anymore

rearing over the water in wind-swell

tuning the tine music of consciousness
awake though dreaming
men rap about trout, fresh water for thirst
cool, delicious

o, of the sky, the woods
strain as hammers drum hollow the log
chant but wordless
to the beat of sweat slipping into earth
wordless sounds beginning to float
air made warm by sun and grebe breast
ruffled by turtle rising to surface
frog caught by a foot in the snap

rainbows have cleaned the sky
of storm
for a while, once again

^^^

Salli shall negotiate
but not the woods, not the ponds
certainly not the boundaries left
between home and Florida
. . . as Molly charged the French
Salli will charge in smiles, painted
as if war were inevitable; her vision

has no thought of French or boundaries
having heard her father's prayer, watched
and learned, her mother weave a black-ash basket,
having braided Jaz and Lucy's hair
her negotiation, creation
gives breath to stuffed owls, plaqued bear heads
rainbows painted double over her long hair
and her young daughters'

^^^

Lloyd heaves, and Steve and Barry
the dug-out is photographed, tethered
now to shore; and Mike holds up freshly caught trout

breathing is heavy, the tramp along the rim
of the twin ponds and down wooded hills in the forest
old men should sit in the shade
contemplating grandchildren and songs, what's on the stove
        for his supper
breathing is heavy, history enticed
blood to surge and lungs expand, old
men should be content with rainbows doubling
Akwesasne, rivers with ocean liners, tankers
mountain ponds stand deep in the memory
collective and single . . . voices shuddered
through egret feathers, bear growls
o, yes, o, remember
(the Eagle will buzz tonight, Deb dance,
Barry and Lloyd, Salli will raise "sprite"
Diane laugh at the virgin)

        in the mud:
                bodies forgotten
                fingers toes jaw spine

        formless words, says the voice

rainbows doubled the afternoon
in Lucy's smile, Jaz's laughter
double the sky . . . "right over the Credit Union"
Salli exclaimed while dodging raindrops

osprey dive, and deep deep in the woods
bear, fat on summer honey, stands straight
elm could not be taller touching sky
lean to tip a mountain peak, bear stands straight
as an arrow piercing lowering clouds
and a bird-cry brushes leaves of oak
perhaps bluejay or raven
as wolf trots through green shadows
burrowing rabbit as raccoon stands erect knowing
summer can be fatal as arrow rips
progeny, tear of breath and guts left for ants
maggots while tail turns in the wind, high or poled
or the cap of a child testing winter

∧∧∧

"Get to the story"

        I am the voice
surely there is a story about all this

            wordless, formless, windless but sounds
            winter and snow is falling
            wood is chopped, corn and venison dried
            muskmelon stored away in coolness
            bear snores in some den (Ray lights his pipe):
            (tehanetorens)
            the children have commenced to nod
            full of dreams and rainbows
            cocacola and fudge popsicles

        "get to the story"

four men
not those who came to take the boat
return the canoe home

       warm lodge sealed at the cracks
       pot-belly stove stoked by Elmer
       ol' rabbit dog, paws hiding his nose
       Francis steps into the room
       holds a pot of corn soup his mother cooked

       four men

       warrior and prophet; poet and singer
       Francis takes a seat on the floor, smiles
       handsome new grey shoes resting beside him
       Salli's two rainbows, a flower and a light, giggle
       dressing and undressing corn dolls
       Kaherawaks munching currants, testing mama
       with a wry smile, grins; Stacy and Ash
       licking stamps for an album
       Francis clears his throat; Ernie clears *his* throat

       four men

       "get to the story"
       "too much description"

       Francis clears his throat, again
       Ernie clears his throat, again
       Louie starts another record as Jake takes
       a place by the closed door near Tom, now
       Kahionhes illustrates the scene as smoke
       curls through the chimney into darkness
       night, story-teller is ready, now
       winter

    ^^^

four men
not those who brought home the dug-out
clans, drawn lines between
corn, bean, squash
charcoaled into vision, photographed
(and she smiles knowing she brought them home)
the men,
warriors or seekers, ambassadors or merchants
defenders, fathers and lovers, lawyers and
hunters hollow log, dug-out ghost returned
again cargoing a parfleche of stories
for winter nights when owl sleeps and snow
decorates pine lifting gently in winds
song over fire in the house

       absolved;
            resolved

       air/drum/water

       voice: get to the story

       ^^^

we believe there might have been four men
the dug-out is large enough to safely
comfortably accommodate four men
(and four men brought it home)

       Peter tells a better story
       coyote howls on the hill
       voice: "get to it"

       morning is something you cannot squander
       cap in a little sweetgrass basket
       however red with strawberry

it is a long story
taking many winter nights
maybe four hundred years
maybe five hundred

and
there were coots and grebes, mallards and loons
the loon sang the loveliest
geese v in precision
and titmice and woodmice
remember muskrat, turtle
wolf howled, dropping pups on mountain sides
there were coots and grebes
salmon and trout in each river
pitcher plant for the common cold
and her shadow against the sky
falling, falling

four men

"tell the story"

afternoon is something you cannot squander,
may I have a drink of water
       may I smoke a pipe
              first

the wind blew open the door, Jake closed it again
a hush fell heavily upon the room

      I knew the great eagle should perch
      upon the highest pine . . . his sight is best

a woman entered and passed a plate of corn bread

      may I have a drink of water

I knew the eagle should perch
upon the white pine . . . it stands the tallest

Kahionhes frantically illustrating, and Donald

may I have a drink of water

leaves have turned golden now, birch maple oak beech
russet, burgundy . . . marsh hawk hunts
bobcat sleeps on the stout limb of the bending sycamore
pitcher has been picked and stored for winter use
night not yet a threat
sun wanders through oak branches
as though looking for the early moon to rise
take watch over the darkening woods

        Eva and Nancy pass the water bottle
        Eva has carved it a turtle
        Nancy, hands clenching chicken feathers.
                moves in words clothed in ancient tongue
                silent music threads the night from Nancy's lips
        Francis clears his throat; Ernie clears his throat
        Danny lights a pipe . . . his wolf robe thrown
        about his husky shoulders, he lights a pipe
                (Rokwaho) (Karoniaktatie) (Tehanathle)
                        (Aroniawenrate)
                (Kawennotakie) (Tekanwatonti) (Kaharawaks)
                (Kawennatakie)

teionkwahontasen

sweetgrass grows around us

    Alex chops cannibals for a boiling pot
    Donald writes lines on the sky
    Mary braids a sweetgrass basket

wind as though from an eagle's wing fans the room
fire lips in the pot-belly stove, ol'
rabbit dog sniffs, mumbles and sleeps
Elmer stokes the fire
Susie teases the poet to write a poem
as Jake and Ron and Tom Julius again
close the door that wind has opened
Danny lights his pipe . . . smoke rises
from the bowl. Carved head of a bear

may I have a drink of water

here are fish for supper
words for your mind
blood for your fire

may I have a drink of water

a face stares through the window, long
hair hangs down the skull, lifts in wind
its cold eyes
stare at the woman,
huddled in a bear robe, her hands clutching greens

tell the story:

twisted, tongue hanging on the chin
splashed in blood
owl awakens though snow still falls
burdens the light

^^^

it was a beautiful afternoon
bronzed and reddened
dark clay darkened in the kiln
roped in circles by strong hands

that could slit open the belly of a deer
praised and thanked
with one tug of the knife
it was a beautiful afternoon
coots and grebes, salmon and wood anemones
trembling in the colors, the brilliant colors of the winds
day shimmering like the first day
rainbows sparkling on every drop of dew, prisms
canoe readied we stocked with provisions and furs
and extra moccasins, beaded and resplendent
no sign of thunder, no sign of rain
corn up, we knew it was safe to travel
rivers even now . . . no more spring floods
past time for strawberries yet too
early for blueberries it was time
four men
        father two brothers and an uncle
weapons ready for defense or revenge
presents for any foreigner
skins of water for whatever march, parched corn
dried meat, maple hunks, pheasant feathers
no one knew how long the journey might take
prayer sticks, beaded belts
winds were calm, water smooth
as weathered bone antler rubbed by winter winds
we were prepared

ah men *onen*
one trillium bloody red, guards
one vine trails off into the unknowable distance
one jay peeps as eagle ascends to the pine

        ∧∧∧

        the story begins

story has long ago begun

it's continuous
in the bear robe warming the old woman's shoulder
in the wolf robe on his husky shoulders
in the turtle rattle held in the other's hand
in the pencil held by Tahonathle
the currants Kaherawaks munches
the eagle's eye, hawk's scat
story has never stopped

it streams down the handle of the war club
it is caught in the grip of the Great Law
it murmurs in the song of the singer
the pounding of the drum, the arch of the carver
the cry of every child, the poet's pen
the raised foot of each dancer who touches earth
and moves as the squash vine moves, as wind
it is the ever-widening circle of the village
and the fire in the house
its narrative is the string of fish caught
the tongues of elk, the belly of moose
flight of northern geese
the color of the meadows and the meadows flowers
the sweet berries and the bitter of sumac
it is the greeting of morning
it is the hope for a good mind

story are clouds, grebes and coots
partridge drumming the earth, loons singing,
and where humans heard partridges drum
it is the flow of the rivers, crystal of lakes
it is this canoe, hollowed and safe for journey
it is the mind of humans, the joy of the child
the journey

story has never stopped
a chain of days, night
following night on bat wings, or moons

it is the eastern dawn, the grave on the mountain
it is the mountain. it is time itself whatever time
may be, it is the budding of the beech
and the falling of the leaf, whistle of the wind
it is toothless old men, or old women
who no longer hear, spittle of the sick
it is the fisher at kill, hawk
the birth of groundhog
it is the fire, this fire flaming
in the pot-belly stove stoked
and the ol' rabbit dog asleep beside it
it is the narrative of nations, nation
and history and circles of the trees
circles
      four men
voice: winter and story moves in the ripple
in Salli's braids; Ernie clearing his throat
Francis' new grey shoes
the ragged wolf robe tossed about Dan's shoulders
Peter's coyotes
yes, I see, I understand
I will listen, I will listen

     now, first, may I have a drink of water

   ^^^

my mother is a turtle
my mother is a fish
my mother is a muskrat
my mother is a beaver
my mother is a boat
my mother is a reed
my mother is my mother
and all her parts are me

my mother is a fish

my mother is a reed
my mother is corn and bean and squash
my mother is sumac and smoke
my mother is honey
my mother is a berry on the bramble
my mother is the sap of the maple
my mother is a boat
my mother is the rapid in the stream
my mother is the wind
my mother is a coot
my mother is a bear
my mother is this house
my mother is the fire
I am my mother and my mother is me (I)

my mother is a fish
my mother is a bone
my mother is yarrow
my mother is hawk-weed
my mother is a deer
my mother is a snipe
my mother is a blue heron
my mother is a yellow rose
my mother is a sprig of mint
my mother is a birch
my mother is a cedar
        that sings in the wind
my mother is a cloud
my mother is a star
my mother is a dream
my mother is a grave
my mother is a wolf
my mother is water
my mother is loam
my mother is fire
my mother is wind
my mother is a fish

I am my mother and my mother is me (I)

and this is the story of four men
who boarded a boat so many years ago
fog has covered footsteps / wind drowned voices

      ^^^

voice: a fingerprint rests upon the wood
etched, a hair still clings
a speck of blood remains a vibration
stirs the pond, reverberation brushes
the softness of the forest

      we're pretty sure it could hold four men

I could feel the sliver quiver on my palm
will I dream tonight
Don't speak of dreams and presences
I just get nervous when someone brings them up
Can't we change the conversation

           O, he died
           I knew, he'd die
           as though, I, willed it

I hold it firmly on the palm of my hand
and watch it quiver almost turning
Louie can record the dream
           and Lloyd d.j. it on the air
Can we tape the voice, voices, I hear
the sounds of the paddles, water, whish as wood
slits through the calm as geese spring

           Francis clears his throat; Ernie clears his throat
           Kaherawaks munches currants
           Lucy and Jaz giggle

as Florence places a bowl of frozen
strawberries on the morning table

I suggested the eagle

yes, leaves have turned golden and russet
marsh hawk hunts as bobcat sleeps on the stout beech
the hollowed log, ghost canoe of men
slithers down water
silent under wings and sweet gale, silent
as it passes over grayfish, sleek bass, scuds
slinking off from the canoe's wake, silent men
as a dragonfly browses the corners of morning
paddle the swift and quick waters dedicated to motion
directed by need and falling light
to harbor before dark and a meal of parched corn
spirited by necessity to seek home
approval of the elders, of the women
warmth of spouse, laughter of children, bed for exhaustion

is their cargo news or merely pelts
or deer meat from the hunt
is the cargo scalps and victory songs or
the decomposing corpse of a son, friend
bones
Don't ask me what I dream
Salli and I both light cigarettes
Lloyd lights one, too
Barry puts his camera away
Steve stands, quiet and deep
Don't ask me what I dream
Everytime I dream
                                    (he died)
I won't remember
Don't forget the pitcher plant
it's growing all over the woods
my mother picks it for the winter

my mother is a fish
my mother is the sky
my mother is a brook
my mother is a rainbow

my mother is a dream
my mother is a drum

bones and shells rattle in the dream
blood splattered on the kitchen floor
a car smashed-up on the highway
Don't ask me what I dream
Salli and I light cigarettes
smoke trails out the open window
as her car speeds towards Malone, the rezz

Danny stands above the river, his daughter
chases butterflies and picks fistfuls of asters
Alex stands above the river on the opposite side
painting a man standing above the river on the same side:
Francis clears his throat
Peter tells another story
Diane smiles at the Virgin, the lie he told her
Priscilla reads her newspaper
a European, Greek, tanker moves down the St. Lawrence
Cornwall Island is smogged in pollution
Alcoa is getting richer, and Reynolds, and Chevrolet, too
someone plants poplars that won't grow along the riverbanks
and trees die in the pollution

Salli and I light another cigarette
Danny stands above the river
behind him his mother braids a sweetgrass basket
for spring strawberries
teionkwahontasen
Ernie clears his throat holding a fan of prayer feathers
Francis clears his throat to give the greeting

my mother is a cedar

Alex paints the river
Peter tells a story
Lloyd builds another tower
Donald writes upon the sky
as his father holds it straight for him
Ray lights his pipe
a bear munches suet in the woods
goldenrod is flowering

Four men
reaching home, reaching
their secret
>   *I suggested the eagle because it has the best eye*
>   *I suggested the white pine because it stands the tallest*
>   *may I have a drink of water*

their secret, message

Wind rises, river darkens
Alex paints the man
Danny lifts his wolf robe
opens it for all
Salli smiles as we drive into Malone
she'll negotiate
I'll try to tell this story

Later,
they found a smaller canoe

"To Be Continued . . . "

UNCOLLECTED POEMS (to 1991)

I SEE WITH MY OWN EYES

For Pedro Bissonette

> *The maker of this song, while in the spirit world, asks and receives from the Father some of the old arrows.*
> —*James Mooney,* The Ghost-Dance Religion and the Sioux Outbreak of 1890

Give me the arrows.
They have come,
They have come.

Grey lights up the sky,
Earth yawns.

Give me the arrows,
Father, give them to me;

Rivers flow, ribbon
The cottonwood valleys;
Tipis rise against the dawn,
Against the dawn.

They have come;
I shall eat pemmican.

> "At one time, I thought all I could ever be is drunk. When I found out I could fight for my people, I became a man." —Pedro Bissonette.

I became a man,
And blood flowed through my fingers;
I stepped on paper flowers,
I walked among wreathes.
Give me arrows!
The herd blazes gold in the morning.
All I

could ever be
           ever be
                      is a drunk, is a drunk.
They have come, they have come.
Father, give them to me.

I grunt in his grunt,
And lay off my clothes
So that the hoof
Could trod my flesh.
All I could ever be . . .
I heard Crazy Horse,
I hear Rain-in-the-face
           ever be.

Deliberate aim . . .
Brain crushed, breast crushed;
Into the wind swept dust
Of empty prairie,
The dried river with leafless cottonwoods.
The herd thundered through
The paper flowers of my grave.
Give me arrows!
I found out I could fight for my people.
I found out
      I could fight
           for my people
                 people!

I went to the mountain,
I went to the Spirit
           of the sky,
           of the river.

I stood in the sun . . .
           hungry, thirsty . . .

To await the dream.
The mountain rumbled;
Springs broke open from the rock;
I drank clear water.
Dizzy in the sun dream,
I became a man.
I see with my own eyes.

When I became a man I became a shadow;
When I became a shadow I became a light!

There is a dry river,
A felled cottonwood,
An empty prairie,
An open grave . . . !
There is a saloon in Tulsa,
A jail in Denver,
A welfare office in Oakland,
A grave in South Dakota.

All I could ever be is a drunk
                    a drunk . . . !

Now in the lands of the Father,
I call out:
Give me the arrows.
I will place them in hands
Not to avenge blood
But to keep strong hearts;
I will place the arrows in hands
To hold the lodge,
To hold the sacred tree,
To tighten the sacred hoop
Surrounding the holy fire;
And in grey and toothless age
Smile upon the young
As they walk, hungry and thirsty,

In the face of the sun,
In the embrace of the Spirit,
The Father,
To the holy mountain
To have their dreams,
They, who will become men
For the people

Give them the arrows
                        the arrows.

They have come
                they have come.

I see with my own eyes!
(*Akwasasne Notes,* Spring 1974)

ICARUS

Out of strange
mystery,
pain of magic
word slipped
tears to his
spring cheeks.

The global world
damaged,
behind his glasses
held in wintered
hands though
october
had not colored
august,
leaves this sapling
maple

would not for years yet
be ripped from his
calendar.

it is good
to know, re-assur-
ing, youth
still cries

FOR BRETT

He spotted them
committed a ceremonial
dance
around them,
knelt
leaned
wet his lips
pressed
the trigger
and shot.

Click
and for a very
long time
the black-eyed
susan
would gloss
on the paper
and perhaps
never
wither
into autumn.

He had leaned
into

something
precious,
something
inexplicably
complex.

RECUERDO

One . . . Crossings

A prune.
Humped in the front seat.
Passenger.
To July Highways,
hot winds
blowing.

A Yuma Dairy Queen
revived life
even
in the noon sun.

Two . . . Pima

rain by magic
. . .
rain by song
. . .
rain by colors
. . .
rain by dance

mountain moves
gives space to clouds

rain by magic

. . .
rain by song

Three . . . Tucson

1.
What I remember are the
    opals
spilling from the hide bag . . .
a deer-skin medicine
    bundle . . .
onto dark mahogany . . .
one rolling into a stain
of the grained wood
by a beer mug.

I remember the pistol
he took from the holster
strapped to his chest
Gently placed on the wood.

I remember my fear
running hot down my belly
running cold across my
    cheek.

Electricity crackled night

without a cloud in the
    sky . . .
in fact, the sky glittered
stars hanging low
over the sprawled city.

He chose one perfect opal
blue and pure,
placed it in my palm.
He picked up the gun . . .
    which surprised no one at
    all . . .
strode toward the door,
    swirled
around and eyed me
in a cavalry glare . . .
"I'll see you in L.A."

2.
What I remember most
    clearly,
vividly than any other
impression is the phone call:
Careening out
the Indun bar
with his friend.
Both a little drunk.
The car drove aside the
    curb.
Seven. Young. White. Boys.
Blaaaaaaaaaaaaaast.
Manny and his friend.
Crumbled into their blood.

I'll sing this Papago song:

        pollen for your eyes

            tobacco for your
journey
        for your eyes pollen
        for a good journey
tobacco

The Arizona moonlight
now
falls into emptiness.

3.
Another memory. Sherds.
Broken on the desert.
Ancient as the mountains
rising from the floor
of the earth outside the city.

Gathered in a grass basket.
Kept safe from tourists
who would desecrate
    meaning
as they have desecrated
petrified wood,
paint of the desert,
kachina,
voice of Geronimo,
mountain moon,
old blood and old rain.
Sherds. Painted in thunder
    and wolf.

4.
To the woodlands
    man . . . humidity.
To the woodsman . . . rain
spring colors of cactus
    blooms.

The first Navajo taco.
First chimichanga
in the pink adobe restaurant
as he sat across the lunch
     table
telling us his wife
was an opera singer in Mex-
     ico City.

Cries of Apaches.
Navajos hunted like dogs
in the canyons.
Carson's
     laughter . . . echoes
forever, reverberates in the
     winds.

5.
Though I have never seen
     them
I remember
her horses
pounding the twilight.

I've read her letters
over and over
so perhaps I have seen
her horses.

6.
Lastly, the night
in an Oakland bar
the young Pima
told me of his country . . .
"its beauties, its beauties."
Oh, the mystery.

I watched him ride off
on his motorcycle
remembering only the
     beauty
mystery.
Hair streaming
long and black in the windy
     wake.

Four . . . Old Coyote

he sings
high
on mountain
he sings

i listen
learn
of centuries

he sings
moon
he sings
dawn follows
follows

once more

he sings
     sings

A Mohawk traveled
     through.

SUNFLOWER

Three summers
it grew
near the black river
beyond the raspberry
brambles
at the bottom of the hill.

The morning walk
always assured
it would be there.

Last spring
wanton boys
found
its stalk.
Summer
this July
will be partially
empty.

They will come back
for the raspberries,
too.

GARDEN

Turtlehead

bloodroot   ginseng
touch-me-not   gentian
arrowhead   pitcher plant
fireweed   toothwart
meadow rue   strawberry

Smartweed

indian paint brush	indian pipe
meadow sweet	heal all

EVERLASTING

STILL-LIFE
For Meg

A rage of yellow asters
bursting light against
the morning wall, truculent
in its beauty orphaned
from field in this city
apartment, sniffed by a cat.

Suns and moons collide
upon the wall
sheen dropping into a bowl
of apples and parsley
green as any spring
meadow or cedar.

Unnatural in its pose,
its place without breeze
trembling in leaves
and stalk, adorning
neither headstone nor creek.

The bouquet in need
of a painter who will
remember its beauty
for a longer time,
its light and shadow
that might remain.

ON THE JETTY
(El Morro on the Pacific Shore)

Consumed by consummation
black wings rose from the seas,
entwined their feathers with the dawn
striking the bulwark of piled rocks.
The wet sun twisted over the horizon
as iron wave after wave struck,
cleaned intrusion from the stones
lifted the moment and the thrill
into the patterns of morning
and wings joined pinions
while day sprang into its usual place.

ESSENCE

I am the blood of this grass
which feeds maggots that
will consume my flesh.
I will return to the field
and my blood will feed
the red berry ripening under spring.

Grass are my eyes
and I view into the years
of desolation out of ruin.
The blood will spill on rock,
dry winds will sweep
its red dust into space.

My eyes are crows
who laugh in the early
of morning slanting across elm
boughs which have no
right to grow in mountain soil.

Crows are my black wings.
Crows are white winter.
Their caw is darkness.
The darkness is the ebony rose
that wilts in the summer hand.

The hand is the receptacle of blood.
From these fingers cries
of creation stream . . . hawk,
peach, the pine, trout
of old mountain creeks.

My mountain is the mystery
of all seasons . . . now thick
in snow, cold to noon,
pink of falling light
striking bare tamarack
and rusting cedar.

Cedar is where my mother
sleeps; her bones brittle
and cracked by rod and spade.
She will never pick berries again,
nor kiss my father's lips.

Berries are blood
thinning in veins.
I will eat grass, gain
strength to combat
maggots buried in muscles
of my thights.

My father will step out
from snow, create
summer of December.
He will replace the grass.

PART THREE

FICTIONS

RAIN

I was only visiting that part of the country.

The Pontiac sped along the back road north of Albuquerque toward the Pueblo village of Santa Ana. I rode with an elderly Laguna Indian woman, her younger daughter who had married an Arab pedlar, her granddaughter who had married an Englishman and her great-grandson who was then too young to marry.

The road edged the rising mountains to the east and the vast mesa to the west. Through the windshield I spotted an ancient pick-up. Two figures stood near it. As we approached the truck I could see an old Indian couple selling melons. The man held one up to us in silence.

In the Pontiac all three women smoked; the young boy drank a Coke. I was thirsty myself for the sweet juices of those melons.

"They look good."

Too late. The driver passed the truck without a thought.

"What kind of melons are those?" I asked.

The conversation already in progress was so intent upon the trip's purpose, our destination, that no one heard me.

"Those Santa Anas are going to dance a rain, I tell you," the elderly Laguna woman announced emphatically.

"I believe you're right, Grandma," replied the young driver.

"Mercy! Hope they do. This heat's a killer. Good thing the car's air-conditioned, or I'd be wilted for sure."

"The juice of those melons back there would have cooled us off," I offered, but received no response.

"We gonna see 'em dance, Gramma?"

"We sure are. See them dance the very rain down, Sonny."

I come from rain country. I wanted rain or snow then to relieve the unbearable heat and the dry sage stench of the desert.

"Alma, when we get there park the car behind the pueblo."

"Right. I'll let you folks out first. And take Sonny with you."

We approached a narrow bridge spanning the Rio Grande

River, which was nearly dry. Barely more than a trickle seeped to the Mexican border at Juarez. A long line of cars and trucks waited at the far end of the bridge to cross.

"Folks are leaving!"

"Hope we're not too late!"

"No. Grandma. They dance all afternoon . . . same as they do at Laguna."

"Oh! They are going to dance down a rain, I tell you."

The elderly woman's face shone with something like ecstatic joy.

"That's power, Grandma."

"That's power, Alma."

"They got power all right."

"We gonna see 'em dance, Gramma?"

"Yes, Sonny, we are going to see the Santa Anas dance down the rain from the sunny sky up there."

"Is there gonna be a rainbow, Gramma?"

"Rainbows all over the desert."

I come from country where it is not necessary to dance rain or look for rainbows in the sky.

"Alma, you park behind the pueblo. Margo, you go get me a big piece of frybread with honey when we get there. Sonny, you come with me to the plaza. They'll find us. We can't get lost in little Santa Ana. I want to be there up front to see them dance that rain," the great-grandmother proclaimed.

Beyond the adobe village an acre of corn, knee-high, sun-soaked, roots scrambling to the river to suck what tricklets of water remained in the August beds. Overhead the clear sky waited for passing clouds. A citron hue creased the horizon.

We unloaded three metal fold-up chairs and an umbrella from the car trunk. Alma drove off to the parking lot. We others headed for the plaza.

At the pueblo edge a Ferris wheel whirled. Music of a merry-go-round tinkled the afternoon. Sonny's face brightened with surprise, but his grandmother grasped his hand tightly. A smell of burning charcoal seamed the air. Young boys weaved in and out of the strolling crowds selling containers of Coca-Cola from large wooden crates. Children, including Sonny, stared hungrily at the various booths selling cotton candy on plastic sticks. A tongue slid along the rim of a lip. Hundreds of people milled between craft stands and beverage counters, charcoal pits were great cauldrons of bubbling grease singed brown tortilla-like bread. Flies swarmed about the honey pots. A leathery-skinned man wavered through the crowds hawking balloons: purple, the color of his lips; yellow as the sun; blue as the clear sky; red as the heat of the afternoon.

We waded through the carnival atmosphere.

In the village groups of people loitered in the plaza itself and on the roofs of the squat adobe houses framing the dusty plaza crammed with the curious. Most people had brought folding chairs and umbrellas to ward off the sun's rays and the rain, should it fall. A man raked the dust clean of the central plaza readying the grounds for the dancers.

People, old friends and new, chattered like mice between bites of greasy frybread with rich honey and sips of Coke. A little girl dressed in bright yellow with matching silk panties showing sat on the dust. A damp spot moved from under her. Two arms reached down and plucked her away as though she were a lemon hanging from a tree.

I was a stranger in that part of the country.

"There's Milly Velarde over there . . . "

"Jim must have brought her from Cuberio."

". . . right under the portico of that adobe, I'm going to bid afternoon."

"Be careful, Mother. These kids might knock you down the way they're running so carelessly. No respect!"

"Can I go?"

"No, Sonny, you stay here with me. Your Mama'll be here in a minute. Doesn't take long to park a car. My, it is hot. I hope these Santa Anas *do* dance rain. I certainly do. Cool us off a little bit."

By then my mouth was clotted with dust. My bare arms, face slowly covered with a fine red film; sweat spotted my shirt.

"Alma! Oh, Alma, over here."

Our driver, the younger woman, had entered the plaza.

Dancers began lining up at the narrow entrance of the plaza between the adobe huts. Women and little girls wore black dresses with red sashes. High wooden tiaras reared from atop their heads over loose black hair. The tiaras had cut-outs of stars and crescent moons. The women carried cedar boughs and boughs were attached to arm bands. The men and young boys were dressed in white kilts with a coyote pelt falling behind, and a wide rope sash circled the waist. Beads hung down their chests. Within turquoise arm bands cedar twigs were entwined. They carried gourd rattles. All the dancers were painted in vermilion.

One older man stood off from the thronging group. He held what appeared a flag pole from which streamed colored pennants. An old woman, obviously the lead dancer, sucked an orange ice cone. She wore faded green tennis shoes while other dancers were all barefoot. She, however, was dressed as the other women and carried boughs of cedar in her hands as did the other women.

"You want a drink of something?" Alma asked. "It's boiling!"

"Broiling," I nodded.

"Oh, glory, yes, Alma. Get Sonny a Coke, too."

"Can I go with you, Mama?"

"Stay with your grandmother so you don't get lost."

Sadly the little fellow sat down on the dusty earth . . . with the sounds of the merry-go-round tinkling in his ears.

A heavy-set old man relaxed into a folding chair next to us. His eyes were rheumy. He was blind. A little boy of three or four stood between his grandfather's parted knees. Both were mailed with silver jewelry.

"It was Milly Velarde, Margo! We had a great talk." The elderly grandmother returned. "Says she's losing sight. Cataracts. But wouldn't miss these Santa Anas for the world."

"Cause they always dance rain."

"All knows we need it," pronounced the matriarch.

"Did you get a look at that river? Oh, my! . . . Look! A hawk."

"A hawk?"

"A red-tail."

"Good sign."

"When they gonna start, Grandma?"

"Soon, Sonny, soon."

"I'm hot, Grandma."

"We're all hot, Sonny."

"Alma isn't here yet, Margo? How long's it take to park a car?"

"She's here. She went to get us a cool drink of something."

The old couple selling the melons along the highway flashed into my mind, my thirst, my heat.

"She'd better hurry. The dancers are lined up to start. And the drummers. Aren't they beautiful?"

"Just beautiful, Mother."

I am a stranger in this rainless country.

I am visiting from a land where it is never necessary to dance rain from the clouds. I thirst for sweet waters of the melons the old woman picked from her wild vines growing on the mesa floor, this dry desert. I am a stranger, but I will wait for the sky to open and flood the plaza, the outer fields with rain. I will wait for the rain to sting my arms, to wet my dry face, to cool my flesh.

"They're about to commence."

A stranger, I spied six men dressed in white shirts and pants join the waiting, anxious dancers immobile assembled into two straight lines . . . female and male.

"Here comes Alma. You should have gone with her, Sonny. She is burdened with all those Coke containers."

"I wanted to, Grandma, but . . ."

"Not much ice in these things. Won't cool you off much. But they're wet."

"That's what's important," Margo commented.

The chatting, the noise of the plaza hushed low. Only the tinkle of the merry-go-round corrupted the silence. We sat there as if figures in portrait, a photograph.

I remember McIntosh growing on the trees back home in

my own grandmother's backyard, and my grandfather's trans-
parents hanging in his now deserted orchard.

I think of spring waters gurgling, spouting from rocky
hillsides of low-mountain country of home, north. I think of
wading in clear creeks coolly wending their journey toward
rivers. I think of rain which will flood those same rivers
rushing to the great lake which in turn will empty its belly
contents into the sea.

The photo remains static. The sun sweats . . . the only
movement of the moment. The sun steadily rises in the sky. It
swirls before my gaze, my brain. It beats upon my face with
hot hands. My shirt grows moist, my face cakes with dust.

I am a stranger in this part of the country. And I am sitting
here under this burning sun waiting for the Santa Ana
dancers to bring rain onto my hair, the mesa cactus, the river,
which is nearly empty, the corn, which is still green yet slowly
parching for want of rain and which will die and the people
will go into winter without corn.

The photo blurs.

Each June my mother would gather her young brood as
though we were a flock of chicks and go off to a distant
meadow. She spent the day teaching her children the rites of
wild berry picking. She would show us how to squeeze the
strawberries and drink the juices under the summer sun,
juices which ran between our fingers, down our arms like
blood from open wounds, and through the crevice between
our usually naked toes. We licked the flesh in laughter, our
thirst assuaged. We spent our childhood in berry fields and
brambles. My mother, however, remains allergic to strawberries.

Later in the summer she would haul us off to the blackberry
brambles, the raspberries whose thorns clutched the skin and
stung our hands with nasty bites and tears. Then blueberries,
currants, gooseberries, elderberries of the woods. Berry after
berry until we had gleaned the land and the wild fruit filled
our bellies and filled glass jars for winter on the shelves in the
cellar.

Rain sweeps across the hills in spring. Furious April floods the valleys. Meadows run black and treacherous with rainwater. The laundry barrels overflow, cisterns gurgle joyfully. Children play naked in the yard. The stench of enclosure, of winter hibernation, is washed from the flesh. We wait for berrytime.

Eventually, slowly the rivers retrench. Creeks babble again. Hay grows tall to the sun, and chicory, wheat, corn, alfalfa shoots to the eye. Squash and bean vines start a steady crawl across the earth. Cows are contented; birds sing. Bears are happy with summer honey. Fox trek across open spaces, tails low to the ground, eyes fixed on a sparrow. Chipmunks race the edge of stone walls of a cemetery. Woodchucks munch grass growing thick and sweet in the open meadow. Then August starts to brown. Wild grapes cluster and purple on vines at the fence.

In my father's pasture an old plum tree hangs heavy with fruit. I taste the sweetness of flesh. It is an old tree, tall and scraggly with few limbs and not many leaves. The dark fruit is delicious. And a pole will bring the fruit down into the hand.

In the winter old men will nibble dried currants and smoke a mixture of sumac and cedar and red willow in their pipes. Women will talk of the largest wild strawberry ever picked thereabouts. Children will crack and chomp the meat of hickory nuts gathered on the floor of the autumn woods. Or pop corn.

The blurred photo swims into focus again.

Sun burns my hair.

I am a stranger here. I have never seen rain danced.

The dancers are about to start.

The drummers are ready.

In the vast, far distance Mount Taylor broods obsidic and tall and heavy against the horizon. A single cloud hovers above the peak. The mountain's sovereign power dominates the desert mesa which appears empty.

The sun blazes, burning flesh and earth.

Men beat drums. The dancers slowly proceed into the plaza. The man lifting the guidon of pennants follows. Two single lines of dancers . . . women, men follow the lead woman in the green tennis shoes. Their faces are stained red. The men's chests are stained blue. The cedar forests of arms move into the centre of the pueblo. Bare feet kick up puffs of red dust. Men shake rattles. Drummers drum. The guidon lowers. Drummers drum even, loud, incessantly. The sun hovers. Light falls upon Mount Taylor. The dark cloud has moved off the mountain peak. The dark mesa clears. Dancers move across the plaza before a silent horde of people. Minutes pass, perhaps hours. No one counts time because time is neither recognizable nor of any importance. The dancers move, interchanging, stepping forwards, backwards, weaving, drumming the earth with their naked feet. Men slide between women to regroup another line. Rattles shake. The guidon lowers again to the earth, the dry dust, yet refuses to touch the earth. Drums drum. Brown bodies shine in the sweat of the dance. Paint melts on the flesh. The sun grudgingly moves before the cloud. The photo is animated before the fierce disbelieving eyes of the crowd.

The sweet smell of burning sage permeates the air.

The crowd is still, breathless. Gnats hang onto the fetid air. The cloud moves.

Drums drum.

A shadow crosses the dancers' faces and the crowd under the umbrellas in the adobe pueblo of the mesa.

Drums drum.

The guidon lowers.

Rattles rattle.

I am a stranger in this part of the country.

Rattles rattle.

The guidon lowers but still does not touch the red, dusty earth.

"They sure have power in this pueblo," the matriarch exclaims.

"That's power, Grandmother."

The blind old grandfather sitting with his grandson between his parted knees relaxes in his folding chair, his face to
the sky, to the cloud, to the expected rain. He turns the boy's
face with his mutton hands to the sky. He mumbles a prayer to
himself and then into the ear of the little boy, and to the
impending rain. Perhaps he remembers his own youth, his
own dance in that plaza year and years before when his feet
were strong and supple, not swollen as now, when his rheumy
eyes sparkled with expectancy and could watch the cloud
move across the quivering mesa to the pueblo, when his
hands shook the rattles, the paint smeared and running down
his chest naked to the falling pellets of cool rain, and his arms
were festooned with the boughs bound in turquoise bands.
He smiled a slight grin showing old teeth the color of dried
corn, but the smile changes into a dark frown as his ear
catches the din of the carnival outside the plaza with the
music of the merry-go-round vying with the beat of the
drums, the rattles, and the pounding feet of the dancers.
What chance has rain with this mechanical noise frightening
the cloud and the spirits of the sky. His own grandchild
begging for cotton candy and a swirl on the Ferris wheel.
His people stuffing themselves with hot dogs and Cokes.
Changes. Everything changes now. He was glad to be blind.
One day soon he would be deaf. Yet, before that biological
change he would start the little boy learning the steps, the
shake of the rattle, help him to prepare the costume, hunt his
coyote, with bow and arrow, and teach him how to forge the
bands to bind the cedar to the arm muscle. The boy would
learn.

The child stood between the knees of his grandfather
shaking a clenched but empty fist as the rain slowly dropped
from the sky.

"Power! That's power," the elderly Laguna woman
whispered.

The lead dancer in the green tennis shoes falls out of line
and accepts a drink of water from a girl at the edge of the
plaza.

Feet move and shuffle.

Red and blue paint run sweaty flesh, mingle, drip to the dust puffing up and flying away from the dry earth.

"Power," whisper the voices in the plaza.

The long two lines of dancers stand like falling raindrops caught in the eye of the camera, a photograph.

Whispers breathe across the plaza, the small village of adobe houses with the beat of the drum and the soft shuffle of feet and the rattle of the gourds.

I am a stranger here in this part of the country.

I sniff the burning sage.

I feel the first drop of rain strike my hot cheek, my earlobe, feel it slide through wisps of my hair.

The old woman in the green tennis shoes leads her dancers into the falling rain.

Dust settles. The dancers' feet cake with mud.

Drums drum.

Rattles rattle.

Rain.

The old grandfather is first to stand. He folds his chair, places his hand in the small fist of his grandson, and urges the boy to lead him from the plaza.

At the roadside I buy a melon. The vendor cuts it into small wedges. I suck the sweet juices, and taste my grandmother's McIntosh, my mother's strawberries, my father's plums. I buy three more melons from the couple at the side of the road and take them back to Albuquerque.

"They sure can dance down the rain in that Santa Ana village."

"Sure can, Mother."

"Mama, there's a rainbow."

"The tail . . . "

And there was.

Down the road a few yards ahead of us walked the old grandfather and the boy in stumbling gait. I watched him turn

onto a path leading deep into the mesa as the Pontiac passed
and sped on.

I am a stranger to this country. I'm visiting a short while.

BLUE JACKET
For David Petty (Dead February, 1992)

1   "They call me Blue Jacket."
    The old man stood straight as though he faced a
judge or jury, or possibly like a potentially mischievous child.
Eighty, maybe a hundred, he had an almost timeless air about
him. Ageless. It was early spring and yet his exposed flesh,
face and hands, was near bronzed. He wore a somewhat
ragged black suit coat and baggy trousers which seemed not
to have been pressed for many years. A single dark hair rose
from a mole on his chin, determined and adament.

"What you doin' in those blackberry brambles?"

Before he allowed me to answer, and without pause:

"I watch you closely."

Straight as Aaron's rod. Not necessarily extremely tall, but
he stood thinly straight, a warrior, a matchstick, proud of his
being and carriage.

"Yes, sirree. I watch . . . very closely."

I could not but notice that his arms—sleeves rolled high to
the elbows—were heavily covered with thick black hair. At
the moment I paid little attention to, really, what appeared to
be fur running the length of his flesh from wrists to elbows,
but thinking back now, the body hair should have been grey, if
not white, for a man of his age. I seemed more struck by the
glint, sharp and penetrating, in his eyes rather than his hairy
arms. My glance moved from his glint down across a wrinkled face to his shoes planted on the muddy ground. They
were curious, the shoes, or sneaks rather: red, raspberry red;
and they looked oddly store-bought new, possibly worn that
morning for the first time, as though he had just emerged

from his winter house and wished to meet the new spring in a handsome manner.

It was early May, the ground was muddy, and I feared his new red sneaks would become readily soiled in the oozing mud. Water squished away from his bulk, thin though he appeared. Behind his imposing figure I could not help but notice his tracks, prints, where he had walked in from the woods' cover. I looked again, expecting to find moccasins, but no, the red sneaks were there on his somewhat small feet, each foot pointed outwards.

He stared me down, puzzled.

"You Indian, too?"

"Yes." I paused. "But not too much."

"Either you are Indian or you are not," he snapped. "Not a little, not a whole lot."

He demanded a more exacting reply.

"I'm Mohawk . . . a little" was my feeble response.

"Aaaaah. I guessed you'd be Indian even if you are pale as the inside of a cucumber or plucked chicken."

He seemed pleased even though my quantum wasn't much in his assessment. "I'm a big Seneca guy. What clan?"

His chest flared. His eyes softened but brightened like the flame of a night candle. Pride shone on his lips.

"What clan?" I thought. It had been years since I thought of clan. Seemed years since I thought of Indian and all that implied. Years since I had spoken with an Indian. Before I could answer, he said,

"My mother was Bear Clan."

I replied my father was Turtle Clan, from Canada. My declaration was met with something akin to a scoff. He waved his hairy arms as if to dismiss me. "I should have thought so."

Before he could ask, I admitted that I had recently, only the day before, come into the area from Ohio, old Shawnee/Delaware territory.

"Delaware." A laugh circled the word. "Delaware. They are all women. We put skirts on them folks two hundred years ago. Still wear 'em. 'Cause we never said those Delaware could take them off."

I had been associated with St. Margaret College near Columbus, Ohio, and was now newly appointed president of the local community college on the New York State Southern Tier at Jamestown. That day, that moment, I was looking the countryside over for a house that my wife, Helen, and I would be comfortable in for a few years, perhaps through retirement.

His mouth puckered at this information that I volunteered. He wasn't much impressed, I could tell. "Teacher, huh," he whispered through the puckered lips.

"So what you doin' in this here blackberry batch? It's the best in the whole state of New York and Pennsylvania. I come here every summer, every July, to pick these berries . . . big as your thumb, round as a full moon, blue as a star. Oh! and sweet, sweet. Sweet enough to tempt all the animals to squabble. Yup, I pick every season."

There was some question in my mind as to what the house owner might have thought of this statement about picking his berries. I knew that it would not please me much should I purchase this place and move in. "The owner doesn't care?" I asked.

"Not much . . . I guess."

He raised his right hand with two fingers curved as if to pluck a ripe berry from the bramble, the thorns gripping the cloth of his black jacket. I noticed long yellowed nails, thick hairs on the hand's knuckles.

"You gotta share . . . if you move into this house. He always did, even if he didn't want to share. Birds know when to get here, ya know."

"Well, I'm only house-shopping. I've several houses to look at and my wife, well, she has the final decision on what we buy."

He had paid no attention to what I said.

"You gotta share. Don't be greedy. I'll share with you. I don't even know you. Here I am talking to a stranger that don't even

live on this property. You will," he pronounced quite empa-
thically. "An' I'll share. Don't be greedy . . . even if you ain't
much Mohawk."

I had to smile.

"Been comin' down here for long time now. Probably won't
stop comin' down even if you do buy this here house."

He patronized me.

Shifting his stance, water still squeezing out of the mud
around his red sneaks, he assumed a superior attitude: "I talk
a lot. But I got the right—at my age. And I can. I'm a big
Seneca guy. Seneca folks like to talk. They say we're pretty
good at it. We learned that in council. You can pick those
berries—the blue, the black, the red—if you get up before the
birds an' others. They'll outsmart—every time you think
them berries are ripe and ready, and you gotta can swinging at
your beltside. Well, they'll outsmart. What kind, Not-so-
much Indian, you say you was?"

I couldn't help but smile. He teased in good Iroquois
fashion. He was testing.

"You a damn Catholic, too? You believe in Jesus Christ? You
go to Sunday church? You know the prayer, the Book? You
know what a Quaker are. . . . "

He did not expect an answer. He wasn't really asking
questions but making statements.

"My wife, Flower-who-sleeps-in-winter—hell, darn, that
wasn't her name at all. Her white name, her white name was
Maud Parker. An' my name ain't Blue Jacket. I just made that
up to scare you a little, stranger. You might think I was the
famous Red Jacket . . . my ever-so-great uncle. Remember
him? He liked to talk a lot. They called him Windbag, or He-
that-fills-the-air. Great man, my uncle. Remember him?"

I couldn't agree more. Red Jacket was famed across the
world as one of the greatest of orators. Every schoolchild
knew this fact.

"What's your name, Not-so-much-Indian?" He didn't stop
to hear my reply. "My Maud was the one who said I talked too
much. If I worked the way I talked, I'd get the work done. Why

hell, damn, I don't want to know your name. You got a name now: Not-so-much-Indian. I only wanna know if you'll share these blackberries when you buy this house. Share with the birds, an' the others."

He stared me down. Stood his ground, eyes piercing my very soul, or morality, or sense of fair play. But if I bought this house, this land, these couple of acres that came with the berry canes, then why should I have to share with anything, birds or whatever? It was mine. I could let the bloody berry rot if I were so inclined, no? He wanted an answer. He was deadly serious. The comic had disappeared. The glint in his eye held no laughter now. I opened my mouth, but as the words slid off the tongue he turned and left, left me holding the words on my dry tongue, stymied. He disappeared. Sort of vanished in the dark tangle of woods beyond.

Straining, I caught a glimpse of him striding through one small clearing after another in the forest, hunched over as if at any moment he would drop to all fours and amble away content in his purpose of the morning.

Chuckling, with a small grin almost of disbelief, I strode away from the thick, wide berry patch that rose out of the rich earth just off from the running creek not far from the house I was considering. Surely this creek, or brook, held trout—rainbow—that would be tasty when sautéed in a frying pan. Trout was my second passion after blackberries.

2 It was true, a fact, I must admit honestly, candidly: I have a strong passion for blackberries. The most delicious of summer fruits, seed or no seed. Succulent, sweet as honey, healthy. I longed, now that I had seen this remarkable stand of canes, to stuff my stomach with the delectables. Old man Blue Jacket obviously had the same passion. I was consumed by it. I had never lived any place in the Americas where I was in complete possession of such a patch. Store-bought berries never satisfied my passion, my abnormal craving for the wild berries. There are those who crave cigarettes or avocadoes, or orange juice, or even heavy gravies.

Not I. My only flaw was the passion for these natural blackberries. A rustle in the brush beyond invaded my revery. There sat a squirrel staring glassy-eyed at me. It grit its teeth together, but its lips parted. It sat on its hind legs, tail furred behind, its little claws empty of nut or acorn, or berry. The furry creature dropped his forepaws and stepped towards me, turned on a dime, and scampered off into the thick brush. What was he trying to tell me? No, no, my brother does not talk to horses. Nonsense. Animals do not talk to humans, only cats that rub against your leg when hungry, or dogs that wag their tails when they want to go out to hit the hydrant. But they don't speak except through body movements, body language. That squirrel had nothing to say to me.

Coming through the woods, the stands of conifers and cedars, I could hear Blue Jacket's echo. "Don't be greedy." That would take some thinking. A major decision—whether Helen and I should buy this house—and I was going to pressure her into the purchase!

I was born and raised in the city, in Crown Hill, a crack in the Brooklyn cement. But I remember well my grandmother and old Granddad. Mr. Blue Jacket reminds me of Granddad. I can still vividly remember visiting the Rez with summer moons on the waters, canoeing, and fishing for lake bass and brook trout. How could you forget the wild strawberries and the June festival, or going to the woods with Granddad in late July to pick luscious blackberries for Grandma's pies and jams? All those summer berries—the blue from the Adirondacks, and particularly the elderberry—and the wine Granddad brewed. He'd sneak me a tip from the tin cup out behind his stacked woodpile where Grandma couldn't see him. He'd mumble some special words and pour the wine with a wink as he handed the tin cup into my boy's hands and said, "Repeat after me, *adowe, adowe.* You must always remember to say *adowe,* thank you. Thank you for life taken and that you are about to drink or eat. An *adowe* to the Creator and that which has given up its life that you may live. . . . Gift of elderberry, corn, or opossum meat."

And I would repeat the *adowe* after him—thank you, Bush; thank you, Creator. Then I would take one small sip of the wine, give him the empty tin cup, and stagger toward the house under burning summer sun. Grandma taught that the sun was Brother; the moon, Grandmother; and all the fruits were sisters. Though I was born urban, Grandma and Granddad saw to it I learned a little, at least, of the natural world, especially to respect all living things because they were relatives and they too had their rights under the sun the same as we humans.

My father had been an ironworker as a young man. A Mohawk youth desperate for employment, without much of an education, perhaps two years of high school, he had needed to go to the States, to the city, New York City, to find a job in high steel. He liked the work and worked hard at it. In time, when he married, he proved to be a good provider, a good saver. Grandma and Granddad had taught him well, too. Nights, instead of going to the bars for beers, he stayed home with my mom and tried to learn a little more from books. He'd say "You never know when you'll need to use more learning." Saturday nights he'd take us to the movies. And after our Sunday bath and castor oil he'd take us out for ice cream or some such treat. Never paid much attention to church, even though he had been baptized Catholic. Never put, as he would say, much stock in church going. Best to pray alone in the woods or at the river edge. He always told me that he prayed on the high steel and that was a good place to pray. Not out of fear—my father feared nothing, he was a true warrior and hunter—but how much closer could you get to the spirit world then there on the iron foundation of a sky-scraper? I guess he was a good man. I remember him as generous and warm; though he could tease and test (yes, exactly like Mr. Blue Jacket), he never taunted with ridicule or slander. He was a good man. I wished he had lived.

Mom, my mother, was a different story, not that she wasn't a good woman and mother. She was, but she wasn't Indian. A full-blooded white woman, born and raised in the Brooklyn neighborhood she had lived in when she met my dad, where she eventually died. Crown Hill. She was Irish. My dad, Henry, always said she was more tribal than any Indian woman he knew except his mother. She got fat, slowly, after one day he reached too high to grab a beam. She claimed there wasn't any reason anymore to stay thin and pretty. Her man had fallen from the heights, and she didn't need another. Her big Mohawk wasn't there to appreciate her anymore. She ate chocolate and lots of buttered popcorn before the TV on the couch. She took a job as clerk in a dry cleaner store. And she never went back to the Rez again. Nor did I after I was thirteen years old.

One night after I had graduated from high school we heard a knock at the apartment door. A man stood there with a Manila envelope in his hand. Mom asked him in and gave him coffee at the kitchen table. I went off to watch TV. They talked a long time, and when they had finished, and the man had left, and had left the Manila envelope on the table, Mom called me in. I went to college that fall because the envelope contained a special insurance policy my dad had taken out for me, for my education. It paid my tuition, and I worked nights in a drugstore and sold aspirin, toothpaste, and condoms to shy, scared men and boys who stumbled up to the counter when they requested rubbers. I wasn't embarrassed. It was my job. My night ended with mopping the floor. I got through my undergraduate years that way. Then grad school—a math major. I'd teach. My Dad would have approved of that, I think. I wasn't overly brilliant, an intellectual. I wasn't going to Wall Street, didn't have either the money or the smarts for either law or medical school. I'd teach. A good career, and I liked kids, students. I have taught math in one small college after another for all these years.

I met, fell deeply in love with, a very pretty girl, Helen Thorne, and have been happy since then. Like my mom, Helen is a full-blooded white woman. She gave me one son and one very beautiful daughter, who, thankfully, has the sparkle of my Dad's eyes, his coloring, his sensitivity, and his smarts. Now both my children are in college and working nights. My good Helen shared all the difficulties, labors, heartaches. She has been a librarian all the years of our marriage. And is a great berry pie maker . . . just like my Grandma was.

Born and bred in Brooklyn, my mother didn't go berry picking. She didn't make elderberry wine. She didn't say *adowe* before she bought a ham to bake or vegetables to cook. She did buy pint baskets of cultured strawberries, and we had terrific shortcakes. And she saw, when I was very young, that I spent summers on the Rez with my grandparents. It was my real college—living with Grandma and Granddad—and where my passion for blackberries developed. Nearly everything I own is the color of crushed blackberries: socks, pants, ties, pyjamas, shirts, car seat covers, my sleeping bag for camping; even the pictures on my office walls are of canes and ripe berries with people picking. I demanded we name my daughter at birth Sweet Blackberry. Helen discouraged this. Later, Tammy thanked me graciously and profusely.

I had to stand there beside this house under consideration and laugh at poor Tammy being named Sweet Berry. Old Blue Jacket surely would appreciate that jest, that honor naming. But would Sweet Berry have been any worse than Dawn or Aurora, or just plain Agnes? Sweet Berry would have been a great name. Perhaps I can tease Tammy into naming her first girl child this. I doubt it.

When the last echo of Blue Jacket's voice and crunching in the mud had faded, I found myself facing the stand of woods, a wide spread of sugar maples laced with white birch, witchhopple, a single spruce, a mixture of sycamore, beach, and tamarack. A young oak leaned toward a white pine, and near the house several cedars stood gallantly against whatever winds might rush off the hills. A mere foot away, a white trillium smiled up at me. A patch of wood sorrel colored the darkness. For a brief moment my eyes deceived me, for I thought I saw Blue Jacket standing pine-straight within the shadows of the woods, spying on me, the house, the patch.

I shrugged, turned with key in hand, and approached the back door. Helen would want a fine report on what the house actually had to offer. After all, that was my mission that afternoon.

I inspected the interior. I was more than satisfied; I liked it sufficiently to bring my wife for approval. Three bedrooms, a study, bath and a half, and all the other usual rooms, plus a small attic, a large cellar, a medium garden plot, a three-mile drive from the college and town, and the closest neighbor on either side no less than a thousand feet from the line. Nothing really unusual, it was built soon after World War II. Neither a murder nor a mysterious ghost hung in the night shadows, or so I was led to believe; no bad spirit rambled through the rooms. Adequate for our needs. I knew Helen would enjoy the rhubarb patch (if the creatures allowed) beside the garden, the day lilies, the lilac, and her hours slaving over the newly planted tomatoes. What totally satisfied me was the study and, of course, the wide and deep swath of blackberry brambles—forgetting the black flies, mosquitoes, and no-see-ums. There were also canes of raspberries on the property, a few blackcaps, and a single currant bush. Obviously there were wild strawberries in the general vicinity, and in the small woods beyond I guessed there would be blueberries and elderberries. I'd make the wine just like Granddad did those years back.

Being something of a prosaic man, as I've been told, I cannot, dare not, wax too lyric. But my heart leaps up when I behold—to copy Wordsworth—blackberry brambles. I could at that moment taste Helen's pies and the ice cream I'd churn in our old ice bucket. Come July, we'd be rich in berries and growing fat around the middle.

I returned to my motel and phoned Helen. She was so excited that she promised she'd drive in from Ohio the next day. I took in an early supper in the local Denny's, went back to the room to read, and fell comfortably off to sleep early.

On rising, I was somewhat bothered by my dream the night before: the berries were all picked, washed; Helen had them between crusts; and I was storing them in the deep freezer. I had the count up to two hundred and twenty-one when I woke in a hot sweat, remembering Helen's words, "Did you pick them all?" and my response:

"Yes, every last one of them."

"You didn't leave any for Mr. Blue Jacket?"

"No. Only the berries dried by the sun."

In all honesty, this did prick my conscience. Had I made him a promise? I couldn't recall. I simply could not remember. My dream was of greed.

My report to Helen satisfied her needs. When we visited the house and land site, she agreed we would buy the place and have an enjoyable life there. When the kids emerged from study at Christmas, we'd hang real red stockings from our fireplace.

On a sylvan May afternoon, late, the sun was slowly wending through the shafts of incoming summer light. In the stillness of twilight, the light yet remained brilliant, silver. There was not a breeze in any pine, nor a rustle of any tiny animal. Perhaps a deer or a raccoon stood off in the darkness below the birch or tamarack in the shadows. One bird sang, perhaps a thrush. I couldn't tell, as I'm not a true bird watcher. It seemed too early in the evening for a thrush. Not a cloud ruffled the sky. Nothing rippled, bent, shook, rattled, or warbled. I had the feeling of home in this silence.

The Buick waited on my cinder drive. I boarded, turned on the ignition, and glanced out the rear window to back out. As I turned to face the windshield, there he was, standing straight as an arrow, handsome in age, peering directly into my heart. I backed out of the drive and raced off to pick up Helen at the town library.

3   She had approved. Had found delights a man would never discover without a woman pointing out those special delights to his naked eye. She found more closet space, a hutch in the dining room, a dressing room off the master bedroom, and other attractions. She sang blissfully

over the kitchen cabinets, whistled about the unusual bathroom tile; she nearly fell to her knees to kiss the waxed and polished parquet floors. She loved the place and couldn't wait for the furniture to arrive from our last home. The garden plot, she aahh-ed about. The front and rear lawns were a decent shape and size. She imagined lovely summer lemonade parties on the backyard deck. She ignored my blackberry brambles. When I called attention to them, she growled.

"They're thorny."

She had no interest. I found it a lone joy.

"Must be a graveyard beyond those trees," she ventured.

"How would you know?"

"Those brambles are too heavy."

I allowed that suggestion to drop. Corpses feeding my berries.

"There is one there." She was adamant.

While she ohhh-ed over the new, bright kitchen, I took a stroll through my woods. The stand was thick but not as deep as I had originally believed. And Helen proved right again. There it was. An old Seneca graveyard reared behind the woods, topping a sloping knoll beyond a rise of green hills. How did she know?

"I just did. I could smell it. I sensed it was there. Call it women's intuition, if you must. Remember when your granddad died, and Jeff March, our neighbor? Didn't I tell you their deaths a week before the telegrams arrived?"

"You're sixth-sensed."

Parker, Jemison, Jamieson, etc., I read and named the stones aloud. Weathered, chipped, some dropping, a few knocked over, names chiselled so light by time that names were fading. On one short stone I read a *B* and then blanks for the rest of the entire first word. Then there were more blanks and the last letter, a *T*. The date read 18 —— and something that could have been a 2 and a 9.

Obviously, an ancient site. No new headstones with fresh flowers. Satisfied with Helen's prediction, I ambled back to the kitchen and confessed to my wife her intuition had hit it on the nail again. Over a beer, my imagination played with the blackberries, ripening, picking, eating. For safety sake, perhaps I should construct a fence around my brambles.

We moved into the house. It all took a good deal of time and energy to settle things into proper places. Helen was most difficult, things had to sit at just the right angle for effect, colors had to complement. The dining room rug had to match the wax grapes in the bowl on the table. Helen said it was good taste, breeding. Time disappeared. Temporarily I forgot my brambles, but way in the back of my mind I hadn't forgotten them. I continued tasting their jam. From our bedroom window I had an excellent and clear view of the berry canes. While stretching for bathrobe and slippers, I could easily sneak a peek.

One morning, to my interest and great surprise, I watched, while stepping into my slippers, old Blue Jacket sauntering through my brambles. He'd lift a cane and drop it, lift a cane and drop it, lift another cane, check it quickly, and drop it. He must have lifted every cane there. I watched him closely for half an hour, then observed him in the woods. I knocked loudly on the glass pane, but he ignored my tapping, stone deaf. The next morning I'd beat him. I was there waiting when his first foot stepped out of the shadows and put down on the mown lawn.

"Good morning, Mr. Blue Jacket." I think I shocked him.

"Oh yes. Good morning, Mr. ah, ah, Mr. Not-so-much-Indian. Out for a morning hike. Keep in good shape that way."

"Yes, me too," I replied grudgingly. Under my eyes, he was lifting the sprays and scanning the ripening process.

"Heard a bear crawling around last night."

"Oh! Where? Near here?" I questioned.

"Yes, up by my house there."

"Where is your house, Mr. Blue Jacket?"

"Around up there some." He gestured to the hills up beyond the woods. His mysterious response did not fool me, nor did it, or the gesture, answer my question. "You live near here then?"

"Not far up there some place near. Nice morning walk. Not far up there."

But not far up where? he wasn't going to reveal his house. Perhaps he was afraid I'd stop by and disturb, or maybe scare, his wife, Flower-who-sleeps-in-winter. I wouldn't dream of calling on them without first an invitation or at least a phone call to announce my visit. I was city born. Thinking about it now, I'm not sure if it isn't Indian, phoning before dropping by.

"Well, what do you think? Ready to pick soon?" Then I happened to remember that I had tramped all over those hills where he had pointed to his house, and I couldn't for the life of me recall a house on the hill.

"Yes, sir, ready to pick pretty soon. Gonna make some bellies happy. Ready soon. Now don't forget to share."

He turned his back on me as if I would not be one of the happy bellies, and he waved his hand good-bye as he disappeared into the dark woods. He did not give me a moment, a chance, to explain my passion, that my lifelong dream was to have a huge spray of my own of these luscious fruits, and that nothing would make me happier. His warning to share had unnerved me, made me downright frightened. What could I do? Well, yes, relax and accept the inevitable. Or, or, I could construct a fence! That afternoon I called the fence people, and the next morning the enclosure was there in place.

That afternoon I strolled out into the backyard for a breath of air after working at my study desk on college papers. And there was Mr. Blue Jacket smack in the middle of the brambles, lifting and checking and lifting. How could that old man have climbed over that fence? It was four feet high, and he wasn't so tall that he could simply step over, tall though he was. I blinked, and he was gone. I blinked again, and he was there again, lifting and checking.

"Mr. Blue Jacket. What are you doing? How did you get in there?"

"Morning. Morning. Nice day today again. Berries are ripening nicely, no?"

I briskly marched to the shiny new fence. "How did you get inside my fence?"

"Oh, I just did somehow. These berries are real nice now. Real nice. Won't be long."

I was so unnerved that I continued to stare at him, probably openmouthed. Words would not rise to meet this outrageous occasion. The sun was hot that morning. Some humidity in the air. With my feet planted by the fence, I closed my eyes, shut them as tightly as possibly, with the hope that when I opened them he would be gone, not there, that my imagination played tricks. I kept my eyes shut for several seconds, and when I opened them up, truly he was gone out from the enclosure and tramping through the woods.

"How? How did he do it, Helen?"

"I have no idea."

"Today's Tuesday. Yes? No? Yes. Alright."

This time he was standing on the outside leaning against my new fence.

"Mr. Not-too-much-Indian, I'll make a wager that these berries will be ready by Thursday at sunrise. Mark it, sir. Sunrise. Thursday this. Some belly gonna be made very happy. Thursday, this. Sunrise." His brown hand dropped a bramble pushing through the fence, and he marched off slowly into the woods, his back bent, stooped. Suddenly he stood in his usual straight stance, turned abruptly, raising his arm to point at the silver fence. "That won't help, much, Mr. Not-so-much-Indian. Won't help." He smiled showing old and yellow teeth.

Needless to say, I was stunned. I actually believed he was going to pick the berries on the bramble that he had held in his hand. But the shocker was when he turned about with his threat. And I knew that somehow he could climb the fence. How, I didn't know, but he already had. A stool maybe. A stone. I was positive he planned to pick the berries. Hadn't he said in our first chat that I must share with the animals? I was, am, willing to have a bird take a few, and to give some to the chipmunks and squirrels. But he meant himself, of course.

And I didn't mind, wouldn't mind, giving the old man some. However, he had said some bellies, plural. Did he mean his and mine, or, or, whose? I must work out a strategy. The fence was not going to work to keep the "animals" out, and he could scale the fence. If the berries were to be ready this Thursday at sunrise, then I'd make sure I was there first. Before sunrise. I'd save him a few. I wouldn't be totally selfish. Share . . . some, a few. . . . Not many. They were mine. I owned that land. For all the world to hear, I shouted, "I'll be there in the brambles amidst the sprays long before sunup when he places his ol' codger's foot down near the first cane!"

I went inside to the living room, where Helen was still arranging the furniture and hanging freshly laundered curtains.

"You are being silly. Plain silly. That old man isn't going to rob your darn berries. There are brambles all over the Southern Tier. He's not planning to outsmart you. Though the way you are acting, he probably could. You're worse than a hen on a nest."

Helen was right, of course. Why would he steal all my blackberries? There are brambles all over the area, rich and thick canes heavy with fruit. He probably has his own patch near his house "up there somewhere near." I was blind silly.

Tuesday passed uneventfully. Then Wednesday dawned. The day was deathly quiet. I managed some work in my study with my eye slanted towards the backyard. No sign of Mr. Blue Jacket, nor even a robin, let alone skunk or chipmunk. I spent the day answering letters to old friends and family. Soon Helen announced supper was ready—a fine steak, rare. She teased about it being fresh game, and the meal turned into a guessing game.

"It's good old-fashioned cow."

"Maybe. A deer peeked into the garden and I took good aim, and now you have it on your plate." She giggled, her fork in the air, the tines stuck into bloody flesh. "Actually, I think it tastes a little like porcupine, maybe bear. Yes, bear, I think."

The evening passed slowly, as they say like molasses in

January. I thought bedtime would never come. I could barely read for excitement.

"Go to sleep. Turn off the light and stop mumbling. I can't keep my eyes closed for your growls."

Before going off to bed, I had left my garden shoes, my pants, and work shirt on the chair near the bed. Suddenly I heard the alarm go off and it was still dark. I had slept after all. Yet dawn was not yet risen over those hills. I knew the old stones in the graveyard had not been warmed by the sunrise. They would be still dark as my backyard. Why was I thinking of the graveyard? Imagining pies and jams and shortcakes, etc., I stepped into my pants. Pulled up the white socks. Pushed into my work shoes, stood, draped my arms with the sleeves of the Levi shirt. It was getting a little tight and would be considerably tighter after Helen baked the pies and cobblers. I was willing to suffer the consequences. I dressed quietly so as not to wake my wife. She'd have no sympathy. In fact, when I told her before bed my plan for the morning, she laughed outright in my startled face and cried out that I wasn't silly, I was certifiably crazy.

Downstairs I made instant coffee. No time for perked. I disliked imitation coffee, imitation anything. I wanted the real. Now I needed the brew and there was short time for the real. Half a cup down the gullet. A faint streak of light struck the low cloud cover. A cold, black cloud. Rain. No sunshine. Good. That would keep Mr. Blue Jacket out of my patch. I didn't mind rain. I fetched the raincoat from the kitchen closet, reached for my flashlight on a shelf nearby and a large water bucket. I'd win. I should have accepted his wager last Tuesday when he stood leaning against the fence. I found a pair of thin garden gloves. I was ready for victory, triumph. I was ready for my blackberries. All of them.

Dew glistened. The morning spit, the foam that we used to call rattlesnake spit, covered the leaves of the brambles, and the spit hung as if a human had passed through expectorating everywhere. I reached the first cane. A few bright pink berries clung to the stalk. No black. I moved left. The same. I moved right. Nothing at all. There was not a single berry of any color or degree of ripeness. I moved deeper into the canes. Nothing . . . nothing. Not a single dark globular fruit. Nothing. Not pink nor red nor black. Light was approaching, moving up into the sky. I could see now without the flashlight. Not watching my feet, I nearly stepped in a pile of scat. Still warm, almost steaming, fresh. Must be a rabbit. What else could manage the fence. Or a raccoon. Rabbits do not make that sort of scat, cylindric like a dog. Must be a raccoon or fox. We'd sighted plenty in the area, one or two in our backyard. Fox eat wild grapes. Raccoons eat anything. Near the fresh scat I discovered prints. Five toes and the ball of the foot on the left, five toes and the ball of the foot and the heel on the right. No shoes. Didn't Mr. Blue Jacket wear shoes when he came to make his periodic visits? Of course, he did. So why did he come here this morning barefooted? As the light from the rising sun increased, I could more clearly see the footprints where they scurried thorughout the brambles in the soft dew-moistened earth. The toes were somewhat odd. The big toe was in the wrong position for a human foot. "Oh, My God!" In the wrong place for a human foot. It wasn't Mr. Blue Jacket, and it wasn't———— Mr. Blue Jacket who would defecate here, in a berry patch.

I slid back to the house for my rifle. It well might be needed. The creature might still be there in the shadows of those woods whose shadows were lengthening across the patch. I had a most unwelcome friend, an uninvited guest. The brambles were high; there was a good growth this year after a strong rain and good runoff. The leaves large, the canes high—high enough to hide him if he were bending over, picking. And he could climb my fence.

Rifle loaded, I returned to the yard. The sun now had risen. Clear, clean light filled the air, streamed through the brambles. At the edge of the canes I noticed black fur caught on thorns. There were many tufts. I walked through the canes. In the interior the brambles were completely naked of fruit, clean as a dog's breakfast dish, and flattened to the ground.

There was not a berry of any color. But tufts of fur were caught on spiky thorns. My canes were ten feet deep, at least, and it took me some minutes to wade through them. They were cleaned, trampled, but all were clutching bits of black hair.

I returned to the kitchen. Defeated. Helen was up, coffee perked, and she had bacon and pancakes working on the stove.

"Well, how many buckets of berries did you pick?"

I grumbled inaudible words. Some of which were curses.

The kitchen window had a decent view of the patch, if you looked kitty-cornered, as they say. I looked for fox, raccoon, or whatever the creature or creatures were who stole my blackberries, my precious berries. I couldn't take my sight away from the window. I ignored the coffee, and it was real coffee this time, and I ignored the food Helen encouraged me to eat. Then, just then, I swore I spotted Mr. Blue Jacket in the canes behind the fence. I rushed from the table knocking over the creamer, spilling the coffee in its saucer. I banged through the screen door and spilled out into the yard. He was not there. An illusion. I'd had an illusion. Trick of the mind. Houdini of my imagination. Optical trick. My depression, my deep, deep disappointment, my painful and costly loss, had conspired to delude my vision. He was not there. Rubbing my eyes, I heard Helen calling from the kitchen door, imploring me to return to the table. My coffee was cooling, and the bacon and pancakes were frozen. Who cared? However, I did return to the house.

"What you think you saw? A blackberry moving out there? Dear, it was just a black bear. Or bears."

"It was Mr. Blue Jacket. I tell you. The old Seneca."

"No dear. That old man couldn't climb your fence."

No response. I slurped the coffee. Her irony deserved nothing, certainly not an intelligent response.

In the late afternoon, having finished off reading class projects for the new semester that was to start the first week of September, I completed a letter to a former colleague, a berry aficionado. It was then time for my daily stroll, a way of keeping the inner tube off the belly, airless and flattened. It didn't really do that much good, but I played the game each day. I got out an old walking stick that had belonged to Granddad, a canvas fishing hat I hadn't much used that summer, put a package of sugarless gum in the shirt pocket, and left the house, avoiding a talk with Helen, who had continued to smirk and laugh at me throughout the day. I didn't need her brand of humor, or sarcasm. It wasn't funny, the loss of my berries.

Out back I skirted the fenced but broken canes, stumbled through the woods, and headed for the hills, where the now western sun had shifted its declining rays onto breastlike mounds. I could easily see the tops of the headstones. That was my destination. Only a few weeks before, I'd been there on my walk. They stood straight. Now several were knocked over. Strangely, the grass and earth appeared disturbed near the one particular headstone that had been so difficult to read. *B* and *T* and then 18-something, and then something that looked like a 2 and a 9. This time it could be read clearly. Not to say I was not utterly amazed. The stone had been smeared with a black-purple juice. The carving stood out broadly in the orange light of sundown. I stared, couldn't take my eyes away. I poked the broken pieces of the stone with my walking stick, lifting some tufts of loosened grass, then pushed the tip of the stick against a wad of black fur. A Canadian goose flew overhead, honked a signal to its followers, and disappeared in the sky. From afar somewhere I could hear a dog bark. Weird, solemn, prophetic. The dog howled. It took a few minutes to find the tracks, the prints, but yes, there they were in the softened earth, the same prints that were on the loam of my blackberry patch. It was then I took a last look at the headstone. It read, "Blue Jacket   Seneca 1829."

I ran down the hill as fast as legs could carry me. I dropped the walking stick. A tree limb caught the canvas hat. I reached the kitchen door. Slammed it shut. Bolted the lock. And stood leaning against the frame, heaving, pulling for breath.

Helen wandered into the room for a glass of water.

"What's wrong with you? You look like you've seen a bear."

There was no answer. What could I say to her. She'd laugh me into eternity.

I didn't sleep well that night.

The next morning on rising I called the fence company to come tear the fence down. They could keep the metal for scrap. When the men had finished the work and had pulled out of the driveway with their truck, I went to the garage for a shovel and spade. In no time at all the ground was cleared and the plants stacked for a bonfire. I wiped the sweat from my brow and neck, and uttered a silent prayer. I was so pleased that I had not named my daughter Sweet Berry after all.

For the remainder of the summer I stayed in my study when not in my college office and kept my nose to the books.

One evening before dinner, Helen asked if I'd like to have a shortcake for dessert with dinner. "Raspberry," she said.

My abrupt answer was simple.

"No."

BLACK KETTLE: FEAR AND RECOURSE
A Documentary Fiction

1   The freezing moon hung over the village.
    Ash and willow were bare. Cottonwoods held but few leaves. The starched leaves, which in weeks past had ribboned the winding creek golden and orange, now were rattled by heavy winds.

A mile off from the village, ponies grazed under the watchful eyes of young herders, boys too young for the hunt or war. The near-skeletal frames of the thin ponies were coated with thick fur. Even the herders' half-wolf camp dogs wore heavy coats and nestled as close to the fires as they were allowed.

Snow would fall early. The narrow river where the camp had been pitched was freezing. The women would soon need to chop holes in the ice to draw water.

Monahsetah dreaded this cold weather. It meant she would

need to go out on the plains and pull roots for the pot, as again food was in short supply. Not only was this her duty, but the belly would grow very angry. Would there be no end ever to this hunger? Would the buffalo return to their lands? Would the pony soldiers and the whites leave the country? Would it ever be easier to endure, to survive? Would the war end? If she lived to be a hundred, she would never forget the horrors at Ponoeohe, the slaughter of her sisters and brothers, the screaming women in the village, the fury and hate of the white soldiers as they thrust sabres into the pregnant bellies of the young women, her own terror as she escaped, eluding the guns and knives of those butchers. It was survival, as now pulling roots from the frozen earth was a matter of survival. Her people could never be out of danger as long as the whiteman remained. Their villages grew larger as her own village grew smaller. She couldn't count the dead at Ponoeohe, but their numbers were staggering. Some people left the village to go north and never returned to the leadership of her father, Little Rock, and Black Kettle. She truly mourned the deaths, and especially that of White Antelope, who was a good man, kind and thoughtful, gentle, loving, and wise. She would even miss Jack Smith with all his brutish, sardonic sullenness. "White Eyes" — that's what they called him. Half-breeds were never to be trusted, although they had all grown up together. They lived in two worlds, half-breeds, never really a part of either, and they were considered as much a cur, a mongrel, as any half-wolf camp dog. Jack's mother's milk must have been bitter when he sucked. But the Bents also were half-breeds, and the chiefs of the band trusted George. Charlie was wild, certainly, untamed, irresponsible — and he always would be. It was the white blood. His father was greatly respected. A man of courage, he had tender moments — a tenderness not passed down to Charlie, who was a ball of fire streaking across the horizon.

She looked up from her thoughts. Day was approaching. Light filled the morning sky. The sun was rising. She watched as men prepared to go to the creek, the Washita.

Though the air was bitter, there were daring men who clung to the old custom of bathing immediately upon waking. Black Kettle was one. He walked along the edge of the partially frozen stream, prompting those too timid to take the plunge, encouraging the bathers.

A child, naked but for moccasins, leaned against a grey chinaberry tree. The boy was crying. The old man stopped and inquired the reason. The boy pointed to the ice forming in the brittle grass that hugged the shore. The chief reared back startled. The boy's whimpering and his naked flesh awoke painful memories. He placed his blanket about the child's shoulders and with a pat and half a shove sent him on to his mother.

The shouts of the shivering bathers reached his ears, and he stared at their frolic. Yet his glance shot back to the jagged ice like teeth along the banks, and he saw a trickle of the boy's blood soaking through to the hard winter ground. The child had attempted to follow his older brothers into the stream, but had slipped and fallen and cut his leg. Now the blood stained the river. The Washita ran red as had Sand Creek— Ponoeoho—four years before.

Apprehensive, weary, the old sachem returned to his lodge. Chilled by the short excursion into the morning cold, he took the horn of broth that his wife, Woman-here-after, offered. He sipped slowly, first blowing on the steaming liquid. He pulled an old robe about his head and tied it around his waist. He thought of the boy, his wound, his blood on the river—only a spot, a trickle. He remembered his young men laughing and sporting in the freezing stream, and his thoughts clouded. He saw these same young men floating on that river, their faces down, their backs riddled with black holes from which blood seeped in profusion. The Washita ran red.

Shuddering, he spilled the broth on the floor. Woman-here-after came quickly and covered his eyes with the robe, and she too then turned to the wall of the lodge. For a brief moment they remained quiet and shielded. The dust disturbed by the fallen broth might well cause blindness. The old rituals were still observed. It was necessary to cover the eyes until the dangerous dust settled once again on the dirt floor. The old woman hobbled off to the rear of the tipi and left the man once more with his thoughts. He dragged the blanket off his head. He recalled that this same blanket, now more brown with age and dirt than purple with dye, had belonged to his older brother, White Antelope. He closed his eyes to honor his brother's spirit. When he opened them, his gaze was blurred. White Antelope had been shot before him while standing in front of his lodge. He visualized the thin ribbon of blood weaving out upon the sluggish current and how it had stained the forming ice. He had watched as his brother slumped into the freezing water, his arms still folded across his chest, his face showing less pain than utter shock, surprise not that he was dying but that his white brothers had betrayed his people. Now there was the child's blood on the Washita.

He called to Woman-here-after and sent her to fetch the holy men.

Though the village lodges were warm with burning twigs and buffalo chips, the pots were nearly depleted of roots. The provisions that the Tall Chief Wynkoop, their newly appointed agent, had dispensed in the summer were nearly consumed. The hunt was poor. Hunters returned with only a few rabbits. Buffalo and deer had wandered into distant mountain canyons to escape the fierce winter that had settled upon the land. The mountains were too far for the weakened ponies to travel, ponies that were eating little more than bark stripped from the cottonwoods at the river's edge. The hunters themselves were too weak from lack of proper nourishment to make the long trek to the mountain preserves.

He would again send runners to the Tall Chief emphatically imploring for provisions.

With her mother and other women and children, Monah-setah went daily to the hills to dig and pull roots, but the stacks of withered turnips grew thinner. They gathered dried sage leaves and made a drinkable tea. They beat the bush to frighten whatever fowl were still sitting, though most had gone south. The women looked to the dogs. One by one, the old dogs no longer strong enough to pull a travois, or young enough to bear spring pups, lost their lives to the empty pots. A woman would call her cur, perhaps first give him a handful of cold bear grease, and then, as he nuzzled her skirt for warmth and affection, she would take his neck between her strong fingers and wrench out the little whine of life. Or she would bash his head with a hefty club.

There in the Washita valley between the northern Antelope Hills and the southern Wichita Mountains, the Cheyenne awaited winter's toll, even though their agent, Tall Chief Wynkoop, had advised them to move out and away from this valley. There was danger. Though Edward Wynkoop could not say for sure just what the danger was or where it would descend from, he sensed an ominous presence of wrong, of evil. The vibrations of this pronouncement stirred throughout the encampment, yet the headmen would not move the village. It was warmer here in the valley of the Washita. The earth's depression and the woods along the shore provided some succor from the cold—surely more protection than the vast open plains on the south, where, yes, they could hide, perhaps escape, whatever evil Tall Chief spoke of that pursued them. Whatever happened, winter with its cold and hunger would claim its due. Children and old men would die of exposure or from the lack of nourishment. An old grandmother who had no young son to care for or feed her would inconspicuously wander, stumbling, out onto the snowy plains and search for a place to drop her bundle near a small pile of rocks. She knew that in fact her people would share what hot broth or dog bone was in the pot with her, but she didn't wish to be an extra burden on the food supply—there were hungry children. She knew that in the spring, when the encampment broke up and moved on, they would pass the pile of rocks and perhaps find her special and curious beadwork and know it to be hers. They would call out her name as they passed either north or south, and hail her spirit, because probably that's all that the wolves would have left, her spirit.

But should there be a bone, a friend might place it on a small scaffold on a nearby cottonwood and leave some vestige of food for her spirit's journey into the world of shadows. She would then be at peace.

Such fears weighed heavily upon the chiefs and hunters of the band, the Hairy Rope people. Yet they had known hardships and hunger before. The people would survive.

Now, however, the village felt the teeth of hunger sink into the very tissues of their bellies. Game was scarce. Not a covey of quail could be routed out of the bush, or turkey found, not even frozen in the snows. Young boys did manage to dig out the burrow homes of chipmunks, and they climbed trees for birds trapped north by the weather. Proudly they ran to their mothers to present the trophies skinned and cleaned for the pot. While the fires cooked the thin stew, an older brother, or perhaps an uncle, angry, grumbled in the rear of the lodge. Once the chipmunk had been boiled with a few herbs and some frozen roots, the mother called her friends to the feast and praised her young man's prowess, and spat ridicule upon the men of the lodge, calling out that if they were women they should dress as such; then perhaps she could find them husband hunters to care for them.

Any and all excuses were taken to celebrate when there was a provider, and the feast, no matter how small on such insignificant game, produced an important support to morale. At such times, good feelings were necessary.

Yet, in the time of the freezing moon there was little to eat and less to celebrate at a foolish feast. Hunger was so great that some women had taken rawhide straps and boiled them down to a nourishing soup. Dogs had become very scarce in the village, and even a boy's pet raccoon was sacrificed to the stewpot. Snakes, when found, were prized, and even the twigs of certain trees were boiled.

Black Kettle expected Major Wynkoop would arrive in the camp with a little flour, a side of bacon, some sugar, a sack of coffee. Perhaps General Hazen at Fort Cobb would have a head of cattle driven to his hungry people. He had sent a small party of young men to Hazen to inform him of the starvation. Once more, he would implore Wynkoop to send seeds and implements for spring farming, to bring men who could teach them how to plow and raise cattle. The buffalo herds had thinned, depleted by both the Indians and the newly arrived white settlers. The people would all die of hunger.

Twenty years before, Chief Yellow Wolf had begged the government to send the instruments of farming, knowing bad days would come for the Wuh-ta-piu. Still the government had not answered the old chief's request. But the whiteman had raised greens on the plains, berries in jars, and beef hanging from rafters. The whiteman had. . . . He had pushed the buffalos away and brought hunger to their bellies. The young men would grow angry again, dissatisfied, when they saw their children and their wives staring. "When they bury the first child who dies of hunger," Black Kettle thought, "they no longer will tolerate this ugly predicament. In spring when the ponies are fat on sweet grass, they will paint the face and the belly that had been full of hunger, and burn those very barns, and probably murder the ranchers." It would be out of his power to stop them. He wasn't even sure if he truly wanted to hold up his hand. There is no way to counsel with ravaging hunger. It does not parley, only cry out pain in the belly.

In the time of the freezing moon, the moon of the mean face framed in hoarfrost, when leaves were crisp on the rocklike ground and ice formed teeth along the banks of the leaden streams, there was more than just hunger in the village to trouble the minds and the hearts of the Cheyenne chiefs. Rumor spread that the pony soldiers would ride to destroy the village the same as they had ridden four years earlier when the Cheyenne had come in peacefully under the protection of Fort Lyon at Ponoeohe, Sand Creek. Perhaps the headmen should give ears to the Tall Chief who warned of bad omens.

Runners had appeared in the village reporting that a great party of bluecoats was assembling and readying for war. Hunters found pony soldiers' scouts on the plains. Travelling warriors, returning to camps farther down the Washita, had entered the village to seek out the chiefs, with information. There was thunder in the north, and the rumbles were heard in the south, in the safe campgrounds between the Antelope Hills and the Wichita Mountains.

Men had been called out to form a war party and go upon the plains to meet the bluecoats. Black Kettle knew now how ridiculous this was. Now in his village there were few warriors young enough to fight, and their ponies were weak. Most of the warrior-age men were out hunting. A few of Tall Bull's Dog Soldiers were at his fire, and it was these young men who called for a war party, to paint and call it "a good day to die." The old sachem knew this was foolish. You do not war in the cold and snow on weak ponies and empty stomachs.

All grew uneasy. All knew some of the young warriors who were still out on war parties in the north, who would return only when their ponies, exhausted in the freezing weather, were stumbling from hunger, as the grasses were stubbled beneath blankets of snow. Black Shield, Red Nose, and Crow Neck were still out. When they returned they would bring many scalps, perhaps a captive, and they would hold a great victory dance. The chiefs knew those young warriors would also bring the long dark shadow of the bluecoats and their guns in pursuit. The chiefs sent messages to these men with word to cease all warring and to return to their home village. They warned that they must travel peacefully through the lands held by the whites and make no depredations. The moon of freezing had risen, and there was still no sign of Crow Neck or Black Shield, no sign of Tall Wolf or Red Nose or Porcupine, only persisting rumors of the gatherings of angry bluecoats:

> We pitched our tents on the banks of the Arkansas on the 21st of October, 1868, there to remain usefully employed until the 12th of the following month, when we mounted our horses, bade adieu to the luxuries of civilization, and turned our faces toward the Wichita Mountains in the endeavour to drive from their winter hiding places the savages. . . .

To decide upon making a winter campaign against the Indian was certainly in accordance with that maxim in the art of war which directs one to do that which the enemy neither expects nor desires to be done. . . .

His [General Phil Sheridan's] first greeting was to ask what I thought about the snow and the storm, to which I replied that nothing could be more to our purpose. We could move and the Indian villages could not. If the snow only remained on the ground one week, I promised to bring the General satisfactory evidence that my command had met the Indians. . . .

I consoled myself with the reflection that to use it was as an unpleasant remedy for the removal of a still more unpleasant disease. If the storm seemed terrible to us, I believed it would prove to be even more terrible to our enemies, the Indians. . . .

I would, in the absence of any reports from him [Major Joel Eliot, sent ahead as scout], march up the bluffs forming Antelope Hills and strike nearly due south, aiming to encamp that night on some one of the small streams forming the headwaters of the Washita River. . . .

One of them [an Osage scout] could speak broken English and in answer to my question as to "What is the matter?" he replied: "Me don't know, but me smell fire. " . . .

The battle of the Washita commenced. The bugles sounded the charge and the entire command dashed rapidly into the village. The Indians were caught napping. . . .

Wrote a disillusioned Army officer: There was no confidence to be placed in any of these Indians. They were a bad lot. They all needed killing, and the more they were fed and taken care of the worse they became. . . .

The plan of [Generals] Sherman and Sheridan was to launch an extensive and carefully prepared campaign to drive the tribes into the reservations set aside at Medicine Lodge, and to pursue and kill those who refused to go. The drive would come at the approach of winter so as to place the Indian at the greatest possible disadvantage.

And as a footnote, consider this, from military historian William N. Leckie:

It is worthy to note that at the time this decision was made no preparations of any kind had been made for receiving the Indian at the reservations.

2 A bitter wind snaked across the valley, driving before it a thin veil of snow. Here and there, in the darkening hours of twilight, snowy whirls cycloned to the steel-blue sky. Five silent men turned up furs against the blustering winds that nipped the ear or muddy cheek, or rankled in the stiffening joints. Drifts covered the trail. But there was still light in the grey sky to show the way to the south.

The old chief rode at the rear of the party. Chilled and worried, he slouched over the pony's mane, his knees barely clinging to the only warm spot in the night, the animal's sweaty flesh. His cold fingers, naked to the winds, loosely held the stiff reins.

Before him rode Little Robe, huddled in fur, one hand touching the icy metal of a carbine. Beyond, Big Mouth, Little Rock, and Spotted Wolf of the Arapaho clucked their ponies on through the blizzard. A mile behind, a few young men followed.

As the party travelled on into the night, the snow ceased and the winds calmed somewhat, leaving only the icy sting of winter. The blue night was quiet and cold beyond endurance, yet the five men did not halt their march and build a warming fire.

It was so cold that leather reins snapped; it was so cold the earth cracked as if a blistering sun of summer had baked and seamed the soil. Frost appeared on the fur of their robes, and tiny icicles hung in the shaggy hair about their ponies' bits.

The old chief stayed at the rear of the party in the hope of saving the strength of his pony, which was wont to lead as if in a charge. Forty miles stretched before them, and the animal would easily exhaust itself too early in the ferocious weather. The old man talked to the beast as it lumbered across the hard ground. In the crust of snow its unshod hoofs beat out a soft, squashing crunch, and the bell tied to the bridle jingled solitarily, echoing over the quiet of the plains like the sad sounds of a sodden drum.

To the left and right, in the distance, on the ridges beyond, came the baying of coyotes. He heard their cries and knew their hunger. This night not a rabbit scurried across the trail, nor a prairie dog darted from its earthen burrow. Not even the flaming tail of a red fox thrust up like a sleek feather from behind a snow-covered bush. Tonight his brother the coyote would go hungry like many of his people in the village. There had always been a brotherhood between the Cheyenne and the coyote. Coyote brought the People from dark into the light of this world. Had Sweet Medicine not bundled the Sacred Arrows in his furs? The Great Spirit had sent this cunning little fellow to traverse the whole of the known world and to talk to the Cheyenne, as the ancient stories told. A warrior society had taken the coyote's name and gave him much respect. Tonight he was hungry, and there was not a berry on the bramble nor a mouse beneath a sage leaf. Like Brother Cheyenne, Brother coyote was hunted down and slaughtered by ranchers and bluecoats alike. He too was despised; he too was an unpleasant disease deserving of the removal that meant, of course, death and extinction. Coyote also was being driven from his winter hiding place. Like *pte*, the Wolf; Beaver, in the streams; Eagle, in the skies. Why was it the whiteman found these creatures so despicable? And the Indian, the Cheyenne? Yes, even the earth that they plowed up, tore up, crisscrossed with iron roads? Was there nothing that pleased the whiteman except the sight of Indian blood on the snow? He destroyed all he touched.

Again the male coyote called out to his female on an opposite hilltop. No food in sight. Only a party of humans stumbling on their horses through the darkness. They were friends. No danger.

Stars appeared in the crystal sky and shimmered in the hard blue coldness. Slowly, moon rose and bathed the night with a pale ghostly sheen. Beneath this not quite full moon, the snow sparkled, icy twinkling in the flow of a fast river.

Once more, Coyote howled, and his cry was followed by the deep whine of a wolf, who also was out in the darkness on the hunt. The wolf smelled death.

The chiefs moved on at the same steady, slow, determined gait. None spoke, nor looked back, nor made a motion that he recognized his trusted friend and worn companion. They barely noticed the ponies' lowering heads and the snorting spurts of steam jetting from their nostrils.

Little Robe silently chewed a hunk of cold, greasy pemmican; Big Mouth, Little Rock, and Spotted Wolf stared straight ahead while warming their tingling fingers within their furs; the older chief, Black Kettle, bent lower over the neck of his pony. The young men following behind had stopped to build a fire.

He was weary. The great Moke-to-ve-to, head chief of all of the Arkansas Cheyenne, the Hairy Rope people, the Wuh-tapiu, was indeed weary. It was a tremendous effort to stay saddled; it was an effort to hold the reins; it was painful to keep his fur robe from slipping off the shoulders, to urge his pony onward down the long trail, this same trail he had ridden hundreds of times since young manhood in war parties, horse raids, hunting parties, that he had ridden hurriedly in escape, ridden joyfully to new spring campgrounds where buffalo grazes and the pronghorn stared down the mountain and elk bellowed through canyons; ridden to offer, to make peace. Once more, perhaps the last time, he would ride this trail south for his people.

The five exhausted, worried men rode to Fort Cobb, where they would appeal to their friend General William B. Hazen, commander of the fort. They would beseech him for military protection. Knowing the bluecoats were marching on a winter campaign directed against the Cheyenne, Black Kettle could only presume out of past experience that his peaceful village was vulnerable and consequently would be attacked. His people were so weak they would not stand against the cavalry's barrage for long. Sand Creek was never far from his thoughts. After a long council, it had been decided that these five chiefs would journey across the night to Fort Cobb. Once more, if necessary, Black Kettle would place his mark upon a paper to save his people. He would prove to General Hazen that he was friendly and wanted peace.

The pony stumbled on the slippery crust of hardening snow. It jolted the aging man; he nearly lost balance. He pulled his furs tightly about his shoulders and stared on ahead, down the cold trail. The wind whipped again into a fury, angry with the night and the five tired humans who possessed it. The wind drove against them.

For a time he attempted to put fears of attack out of his mind. He tried to recall the faces of old friends, friends he had known first when he came south from the Pa Sapa territory. There had been Yellow Wolf to greet him, to make a place at the campfire for his small band, to welcome the young brave eager to prove himself in raids against the Kiowa and the Comanche. Probably Yellow Wolf had had more to do with his intellectual growth than any other man. When young, he had often sat at the older man's feet in council and listened in rapt attention. Then Yellow Wolf was aging but wise. Peace was always his first thought, peace and trade with the whiteman. There had been those, Indians and whites alike, who had laughed at the old chief when he had implored the Indian agents to bring them farming equipment and seeds and to hire a whiteman to build them a wooden village and instruct them how to raise cattle. Yes, many had laughed. And no implements had ever arrived in the wagons crossing the plains. As Yellow Wolf had fled north, now Black Kettle fled south for protection from the bluecoats and the Great White Father who could never understand the Indian nor his way of life. Yellow Wolf was finished: a soldier's bullet had taken him down at Sand Creek, had taken him as it had his friends War Bonnet and Standing Water and White Antelope. Those were bad thoughts to keep alive like burning coals in Black Kettle's mind. Think only of the people still living, hungry and waiting! And yet how fully and frighteningly he realized that the whiteman thought them a bad lot that needed killing. At present they were not pursued to be placed on a reservation, but hunted like game to be slaughtered and nailed to the wooden village walls like the stuffed heads of deer and buffalo trophies. Did not some bluecoat carry in his pocket White Antelope's scrotum used as a tobacco pouch? Black Kettle's anger commenced to warm his body. The sting of the wind did not cut as rawly into his cheek, which now burned.

Moke-to-ve-to had been hostile once. He had painted and rolled his pony's tail for the warpath. He had even placed his knife below the skin and torn away the scalps of his enemies. He had found the Ute after they had captured his first wife, Vo-ish-tah (White Buffalo Woman), and taken her to their village, never to return to her young warrior husband; they had taken her away from him as though they had ripped a rib from his chest, the loin of his thigh. He had raided Pawnee and Crow for ponies; he had attacked the ancient enemy; and it was true, he had at times led depredations against the white settlers and the pony soldiers. They had advanced too far into Cheyenne lands. They had ripped the Mother Earth with the deep blades of their plows. They had driven off the buffalo when their bullets did not stop him in his roaming tracks. They had carried their diseases under their blankets, and they shook those same blankets of disease out upon the people. They gave his young men rot-gut whiskey, which made them mean, lazy, and weak; some young men and women went to the whiteman's coffee pot and never returned to their village fires. Perhaps even worse than those atrocities, they had brought the bluecoats and their guns who found it a sport to kill innocent children, women pregnant with the nation's young; who smashed the heads of infants, raped young girls, sliced off the manhood of his warriors, and dignified old chiefs. These were cruel men, men whose hearts were not sweet but bitter like the gall of their oxen. These were vicious men who wished only for the extermination of the Wuh-ta-piu. Oh, the Cheyenne had been so wrong, so thoughtless, to open their robes to those men! So he had danced in the firelight of the darkness, had thrust the point of his lance into the earth, and had ridden off to battle calling *hookahey* to his followers. Yes, it was a good day to die for your principles, for your blood, for your nation and Creator and the Mother Earth. Hookahey. And so he would return to the village, his face painted black for victory, his hands already vermilion with blood, and would dance the great victory celebration with the white scalps dangling from the tip of his lance, blood still fresh on his war club.

The hunger for revenge that had once driven him to war, now again, on this night of the freezing moon of the hard face, blew upon the old ashes protecting the coals smouldering in his heart. He took warmth from this fire and urged his pony on into the darkness.

One day amidst the thick of battle it had come to Black Kettle that he and his people were to be exterminated by the whiteman. He saw, as in a vision, that all the people had fallen down, and all the buffalo had fallen down, and all the horses had fallen down. The war club beat, the arrow flew, the carbine smoked, but all the people had fallen down. All that remained standing were the whiteman's fence posts, his singing trees along the roads, and the steam from his iron horse.

Black Kettle had turned immediately and had ridden among his warriors calling for a cease-fire to end the kill. He, Moke-to-ve-to, head chief of the Hairy Rope people, would war no more. He would bundle his lance in the skins of coyotes; he would dismantle his carbine. He would break his arrows. He would raise a white flag above his lodge. Not because he loved and trusted the whiteman or his peace treaties, which benefitted only the whiteman. He had watched for many summers the death struggles of all the creatures of the plains and the mountains. He had watched the sharp axe fell the cottonwoods. He had listened when women called out that the hackberry bushes were plowed under and the turnip had been crushed by the pony soldiers. He had seen the lands loaned to them by Mother Earth grow more and more constricted until they were insignificant islands in the middle of the whiteman's sea of grass. He had heard the bluecoats' gunfire and had watched their guns kill his strongest men, his most powerful braves and his wise chiefs. He had watched pregnant girls die, bellies cut open, and the children of his people's blood smashed. He had watched as hundreds died with the blanket disease, and had observed those great holes, the gashes in the faces of those who had survived the blankets' weight. He learned you could not fight and win against the soldiers the Great White Father sent into his lands. They fell upon them like rain but with the strength of a blizzard and the power of lightning. Their flood could not be stopped, nor could they be driven back to their lands on the eastern shores. They sprang up again like new grass after spring rains. Peace must be made. The lance must be put down for the plow, the war club for the hoe. The people must learn new ways, a new Cheyenne way. They must plant seed in a garden, raise cattle to graze. The voices of the shadows came to him. Yellow Wolf spoke, Tobacco spoke, even the traitor One Eye spoke. The People must survive. They must grow strong hearts, strong bodies, strong minds. His young must firm up every muscle of their beings, throwing off the bad gifts they had accepted from the whiteman.

That is why this great warrior, when proclaimed chief, became a man of peace, but a statesman whom the young men laughed at, ridiculed, and cursed. The war lord Roman Nose scoffed at this peace chief and persuaded the old man's young braves to join him and Tall Bull with the Dog Soldiers and the hostile Lakota warriors. What did it get Roman Nose? Death. What did it get Tall Bull? Death. His bones bleached at Summit Spring.

The big soldier chief, General Sheridan, had called him a worn-out and worthless old cypher. Others of his own nation named him a fool. At the signing of the Medicine Lodge Creek treaty, his own men went against him and threatened not only to kill his stock and horses but to take his life. None of this mattered. Nothing was important but the endurance of the Wuh-ta-piu. Not even his death by assassination would be important.

Black Kettle gathered his family and relatives about him. He gathered trusted friends who like himself believed in the peace, and they villaged together. There were those in his camp who sneaked off to raid the whites. One day they too would stop thumbing their noses and slapping their buttocks in derision and settle down on the lands of the reservation at peace with the whiteman.

Moke-to-ve-to had been lied to, tricked, made a pawn in the game of survival, yet he was proud to think he had never lied to his heart, tricked his people, or played games with anyone's life. He had spoken out for war when he thought it was necessary, justifiable; and he had spoken out against war when killing involved innocent people. He finally came to realize that it was impossible to fight the swarms of whiteman. The "pale-eyes" meant to stay in the belief it was their destiny, an act of progress in the advance of their most-materialistic civilization. Not only had they built wooden lodges, but they had planted trees in the clearings where there were water holes. Victory could never be achieved. The Indian would never push the whiteman back to the eastern shores. Black Kettle now fought bitterly, with all the strength of his body and mind, for peace.

For sixty-seven years he had watched the cottonwoods turn green, then orange along the riverbanks, and he lived now to ensure that, for sixty times sixty years more, his people would continue to ensure the greening of the timbers and to feel and hear the falling of the rain and the rising of the winds. He could not imagine a time when the ponies would not grow fat on new spring grass, or the buffalos would not roam the plains, or the wild pea would not flower on the bluff, or men would not ride off to hunt while women waited on the knoll to skin the game killed, dry out the meat, pound it into pemmican with wild berries, and build lodges with the skins. He could not imagine a time when boys would not go to the sacred hill for their dreams, for visions of their future.

The Cheyenne way was good. Why did the whiteman wish

to wipe it out? They had been brothers once, and they must hold hands again.

A gust of wind brought him back from the shadows of the past. Once more he found himself heading south to Fort Cobb:

> I will say nothing and do nothing to restrain our troops from doing what they deem proper on the spot, and will allow no more vague general charge of cruelty and inhumanity to tie their hands, but will use all the powers confided to me to the end that these Indians, the enemies of our race and our civilization, shall not again be able to begin and carry out their barbarous warfare on any kind of pretext they may choose to allege.
>
> (Sherman to Sheridan, October 9, 1868)

> The more we can kill this year the less will have to be killed next year for the more I see of these Indians the more I am convinced that they will have to be killed or be maintained as species of paupers.
>
> (Sheridan)

> The only good Indian I ever saw was dead.
>
> (Sheridan)

The men rode on through the cold night with the young braves following behind. At last the dark sky was streaked with ribbons of light. In the distance the tent peaks of Fort Cobb were sighted.

On arriving at the fort, which was really a supply depot composed of army tents, the chiefs were taken to General Hazen's quarters and offered food and sugared coffee, which they enjoyed greatly, before sitting down to council. A pipe was brought out from under a robe, and a smoke exchanged before the chiefs spoke.

Little Robe and Spotted Wolf spoke first, claiming their rights to the Washita reservation. Black Kettle raised his glance from the cooling ashes of the pipe. He sat cross-legged, his blanket loosely pulled about his shoulders, his expressive hands lightly clenched, folded in his lap. His wise, sad face showed heavy signs of fatigue and was shadowed with a mask of fear:

We only want to be left alone. All that we want is that you yellow faces keep out of our country. We don't want to fight you. This is our country. The Great Spirit gave it to us. Keep out, and we will be friends."

His colleagues nodded heads in agreement. The chief spoke slowly as always, but as if in pain:

My camp is now on the Washita, forty miles east of the Antelope Hills, and I have there about eighty lodges. I speak only for my own people.

Why should the bluecoats attack, as rumor had it? The Cheyenne were there on lands granted by the Medicine Lodge Creek treaty. Grey Blanket (John S. Smith) and the Little White Chief (William Bent) explained the boundaries. The Tall Chief (Edward Wynkoop) had advised against it, but George Bent had suggested the camp there on the banks of Okeahah, the Washita, under the winter protection of the cottonwoods and chinaberry trees.

Black Kettle explained that the whitemen were to blame for all the murders in Kansas. They had fired upon the hunters. He admitted that he could not keep a strong hand upon his young men. They could not forget Sand Creek and lived in dread that the massacre would be repeated. When fired upon, they returned fire. Sadly, tragically, deaths occurred.

Big Mouth, the Arapaho, voiced his fear that the rumors would prove correct that the bluecoats were on the march.

The general listened quietly, intently, to his interpreters. Clear-eyed, not totally unsympathetic, but in full knowledge of their destiny, he allowed his lips to part in a half smile as though to negate the rumor and pacify the chiefs. His thin fingers crawled along his weather-beaten cheek to his mustache, which he stroked nervously. Still a young man, not forty years old, he was a veteran of the Civil War between the States under Sherman's command, and a seasoned Indian fighter. He was still suffering from a wound received from an Indian. An intelligent commander, he was cognizant that the Indians had been dealt an injustice. He was well aware that the whitemen, emigrants and soldiers alike, fervently desired the Indians' demise by whatever means were available. The faster the better. He knew there were commanders in the field who hungered for glory and game, and should the extermination of "savages" be the road to this end, then the road would be travelled gallantly. Under the guise of a punishment expedition, extermination would commence. New stars would rise over the plains.

Doubtless Hazen was a good soldier, a firm commander, and an intelligent man not totally devoid of insight into human misery. Though old grievances rankled in his memory, he could do nothing but carry out orders. General George Armstrong Custer was on the prowl for scalps and recognition. General Phil Sheridan, his immediate superior, was on the march, and his aversion to Indians swept like winter winds across the plains. Hazen possessed full knowledge of Sheridan's march into Cheyenne territory and his purpose. This was not a routine patrol.

He made an attempt at honesty and fumbled with his words in explaining that he could not stop the soldiers from attacking hostile villages. Nor could he promise protection at Fort Cobb. Black Kettle's band, with the Dog Soldiers of Tall Bull, were known hostiles:

> I am sent here as a peace chief. All here is to be peace, but north of the Arkansas is General Sheridan, the great war chief, and I do not control him, and he has all the soldiers who are fighting the Cheyennes and Arapahos.

The chiefs grumbled amongst themselves.

> Therefore you must go back to your country, and if the soldiers come to fight, you must remember they are not sent from me, but from the great war chief, and it is with him you must make your peace.

The worried chiefs all seemed to stare at a wisp of smoke still smouldering in the discarded pipe.

But you must not come unless I send for you, and you must keep well beyond the friendly Kiowas and Comanches.

This offered nothing — wind in the hand.

Hazen stood as if to dismiss the men and paced the small office tent. Turning abruptly, he looked directly into Black Kettle's worn eyes, masking the chief's fear and doubt, which were not untouched by anger and disappointment. He said,

I hope you understand how and why it is that I cannot make peace with you.

He added that he had heard through Comanche chiefs that the celebrated peace chief Black Kettle had lost favor with his young men and that they no longer listened to his counsel nor were under his command.

Black Kettle did not dispute this accusation. He reasoned that under Cheyenne custom he could not speak for all the bands and all the people, that each person was an individual, and that as headman he could merely advise and not command.

To this Hazen offered a frugal smile as he concluded their talk.

Before the men left the fort, the general had sugar, coffee, tobacco, and a little flour given them to take back. Then they were dismissed.

He was positive that he would never set eyes upon the "old cypher" again.

3 Heap Injuns down there. . . . Me heard dog bark

I was rewarded in a moment by hearing the barking of a dog in the heavy timber off to the right of the herd, and soon after I heard the tinkling of a bell. . . . I turned to retrace my steps when another sound was borne to my ears through the cold, clear atmosphere of the valley — it was the distant cry of an infant; and savages though they were and justly outlawed by the number and atrocity of their recent murders and depredations on the helpless settlers of the frontier, I could not but regret that in a war such as we were forced to engage in the mode and circumstances of battle would possibly prevent discrimination.

(Custer)

On the night of November 26, 1868, the moon of the freezing face, the chiefs, when arriving in the village, found a small raiding party there under Crow Neck and Black Shield with fresh scalps. Already they had urged the women to build a fire for a victory dance to be held at moonrise.

During those depredations two Kiowa warriors, just back from a pony raid upon the western Ute, had entered the village and spoke with the headmen. They told how their ponies had crossed the heavy trail stamped into the snow by many horses that wore shoes. Ar-no-ho-woh (Woman-hereafter) offered these warriors hot broth, and soon they left for the Kiowa village downstream.

Black Kettle prepared for the eventual attack. He tethered his best pony to the poles of his lodge. He placed a sentinel on guard and arranged in his mind how he would ride out to the soldiers before the attack and speak with them. He would tell them, his white flag above his head, of the peace in his heart, that he did not want to fight and they should go home.

From a safe distance Monahsetah observed, dismayed, the celebration. She knew they were foolish, crazy what with the premonitions of danger all about. She knew some of these youths, hot-tempered young warriors, knew that they would do as they wished and that her father and the other chiefs had no control over them. It was cold. It was time for her to go to sleep. She closed the lodge flap and disappeared into the darkness.

The joy of the dancers drummed the night. Shadows cast by the fire fell against lodge walls. Black Shield led a young woman by the hand to the dance, and they joined the celebrants. An old woman broke between the lines and stacked dry buffalo chips on the fire.

Black Kettle stepped out into the lateness of the night,

looked up at the waning moon, and shivered. He looked off south beyond the camp. There he saw the small fire of the pony herders flicker. He had warned the young men that bluecoats were on the march. They had laughed at him. They laughed now and ridiculed him for being a worried old woman. They shouted that it was winter, snow littered the ground. "Look, now it's falling," they said, pointing. It was the moon of the hard face. Pony soldiers did not fight in this bad weather.

There was no way he could counsel these men; they had already forgotten that Mashane (Chivington) had attacked the village at Sand Creek in the moon of the hard face. They refused to listen. Black Kettle's admonishments fell upon the snow and were scattered by the winds. Peace would come at a heavy cost, and the night's revelry would be paid for with flesh and blood. He hoped that at least Double Wolf would not join the celebrants, wear out his energies in the exhilaration of the dance, and slip into sleep on guard. This might be the very night the bluecoats were stalking the outlying hills, preparing to creep upon the village.

A dog barked. The tinkle of a pony bell struck the night. The herders were probably asleep. The vigil fires flickered in the distance. He heard the cry of a baby.

Now the burden.

Hearing the baby's cry, he remembered the young child's blood smearing the ice edging the creek. He shuddered and entered the lodge.

PART FOUR

ESSAYS AND REVIEWS (to 1991)

PREFACE: *IS SUMMER THIS BEAR* (1984)

I have never recognized humankind's supremacy. I have never granted humankind that boastful ego. Humans forget there was a time before them, and perhaps shall be a time after them. Perhaps. And though I have never had a particular fondness for the Norwegian rat nor the Brooklyn cockroach, I find it difficult to deny them breath. Someplace, somewhere, somehow they join the family of all creatures and have a purpose in the Creator's perfect design. I would suppose that rat has as much right in city sewers as hawk a perch upon an elm, or wild strawberry in a spring meadow. It has its own set of rules, its own needs for survival, and undoubtedly its own niche in the balance of things.

There is no fear in my heart, however, that either the Norwegian rat or the Brooklyn cockroach will not survive whatever nuclear blast . . . They accommodate themselves so much more easily than the wild strawberry dependent upon clean sun and new spring. I fear more for the survival of hawk, rainbow trout in the Adirondack lakes, pike in the St. Lawrence, iris in the marsh, and bear of the forest; yes, yes, of course, even humankind . . . in its human beauty and human stupidity, creativity and destructive foolishness. I bed nightly in trembles that its foolishness, its blindness will overpower good sense, and that all creatures, little and large, will die. And, yet, is not humankind beautiful, as handsome as wolf or turtle, though perhaps not as courageous as muskrat nor quite as bountiful as corn, or beans, or squash, the three sisters? But humankind has spirit . . . as much spirit as eagle's good sight, blackberry's sweetness, the honey bee's flight. And because of this spirit, perhaps humankind will survive, modesty prevail, and common sense allow all other creatures the justful right to survival as well.

Should they listen to the elders, humankind will be guided to the right path; should humankind respect hornet or fisher or willow, they will come to understand the nature of things and the design the Creator wove into the tapestry of life, all life. And humankind will thank stars and rivers, birds and animals, winds and dreams: turtle who has so long carried them on his shell, and those who shall surely follow. Adowe.

Herein are songs and stories to remind humankind of their beauty and that around them, and to suggest their obligation. Here is the drum reverberating within woods and meadows, across great bodies of water and sky, and in spirit of all kind.

REMEMBRANCE: AMIRI BARAKA

In the spring of 1957 I arrived in the West Village, New York City, from my father's house in northern New York near the St. Lawrence River, to attend the university and, eventually, after study, I would obviously have dynamic fame thrust upon me as a poet. Wherever this foolish, romantic idea came from I do not remember, and it is not an idea, dream, I now pass along to other young student poets. Rarely, if ever, does it work that way. But to tide me over until fall registration I took a job as a book clerk which shortly led to a promotion to store manager. At about this time I was lucky, and I mean lucky, to get a small press publisher, Troubador Press, interested in printing a collection of my poems. I was feeling smug, probably arrogant, and, I'm sure, was utterly intolerable at whatever social gathering I attended.

One bitterly cold afternoon, the sun setting the other side of the Hudson sent mustard rays down West 57th Street towards the bookshop. It was nearly time for me to leave work and I stood counting cash for the night staff when the door opened, pushed by a stiff breeze, and a young Black man entered. He was slightly round-shouldered, from the cold wind I presumed, tattily dressed, and spoke sentences not quite edged in bitterness; not sardonic, but soft the sounds were: there was a frost of unfriendliness in the tones. The front cash-out desk was located near the door, he did not need to step too far into the shop, and something told me he wouldn't have ventured too deeply into the interior anyway.

Without a smile he held up a small grey magazine printed in heavy type in blue ink. The title blazed before me. I hadn't a clue as to what the title meant. He announced it was a new poetry journal, and holding it like a Jehovah's Witness holds *Awake* in subway stations, he inquired if I'd keep copies on the shelf for possible sales. Consignment, of course.

I was familiar with the *Kenyon Review, Poetry,* the *Saturday Review,* and a few others, of course . . . as all young poets of the time were, but *Yugen?* Not this magazine the laconic young man pushed under my critical and uninformed naïve gaze. I said no to his request.

He didn't even shrug his shoulders, but arched an eyebrow, turned and left as mysteriously as he had arrived. In the cold wind blowing papers along the street, I watched out the window the young man disappear into the thickening crowd. He had seemed indifferent to my closed hand, unperturbed by my negative decision, but *sure* in his mission. Shortly, I regretted not having allowed him to leave four or five copies behind. I had no idea where to reach him to say I had changed my mind.

A few weeks later I was on Morton Street with the publisher of my book. Rolling off the press was the new issue of a magazine.

My mind filled with a sudden rush of remembrance of that late afternoon scene in the bookshop.

"That was LeRoi Jones. He edits *Yugen.*"

I was unimpressed. The name did not rime for me with Eliot, Ransom, Hughes nor Thomas, Dylan. I did condescend to read a page or two . . . poems by poets I'd never heard of nor was likely to ever hear of again . . . obviously Greenwich Village hang-abouts who spent waking time in coffee shops or even more bizarre shops of less legal pursuits of entertainment. I was smug.

Brayton Harris, my publisher and the printer, could not convince me of either Jones' or *Yugen's* worth. "He's going to be an important poet one day. His magazine will be famous."

Doubtfully I "yessed" him.

At that moment a young good-looking fellow bounced into the print shop. With shocks of unruly dark hair cascading down his forehead over an oval moonlit face, possessed of a jolly nature, he smiled words rather than spoke them. He immediately asked if I wrote poetry.

I murmured something about yes and sonnets and sestinas and the university.

"Shit. I don't know what a sonnet is. But I know the streets and the people. That's poetry." He arched a shoulder and turned to Brayton. "How's my book doin'?" He prodded with a jovial smile.

"It's coming, Jack, it's comin'."

"He's publishing my book . . . *Red River of Wine.* How's that for a title?"

He really didn't want my comment, but, actually, I thought it a pretty good title. Brayton introduced us:

"Jack Micheline, this is Maurice Kenny . . . You're both Troubador poets."

"Oh Yeah! Kenny." It didn't rime with Keats or Byron. "Yeah," smiles fading, "I saw your book. What's it called . . . *Lead Letters.*"

"No, but you're close . . . *Dead Letters Sent* . . . from Gerard Manley Hopkins." I thought it an excellent title.

"Who? Never heard of him." Jack, unimpressed with the title, the book itself and Hopkins, turned directly to Brayton. "Did LeRoi put any of my poems in the magazine?"

Pleased that his book would shortly be pressed and bound, and pleased, also, that a poem would appear in *Yugen,* he waved a big smile and trotted off, saying he had to get with Jack next door at Bob Wilson's Phoenix Bookshop.

"Kerouac, he means," Brayton clarified. Another name that didn't rime with Faulkner or Fitzgerald or even Carson McCullers.

"I took the liberty of showing some of your poems to LeRoi. Had a guess he might use something in this issue. He thought you were a little . . . a little too regional, rural . . . pastoral.

Too many hawks and flowers and rivers . . . none which carry "red wine."

"You mean he didn't like them."

"No." Emphatic.

Yugen did roll off the press for a few more issues, was distributed, or peddled, by Jones himself walking up one avenue of the city and tramping down the other. He continued to publish poets whose names continued not to rime for me: Kirby Congdon, Gregory Corso, Diane DiPrima, etc. . . . Where were Catullus and Sappho and even Louise Bogan of our own then. Youth is usually stupid . . . or was in those days, and blind. And I was totally without sight, and smell. Arguing with my ego, I decided I didn't want to be published in Jones' dippy magazine with an unpronounceable name . . . I consoled my wounds. I'd wait for the *New Yorker* to buy my unpublished poems. They print lots of poems about barns and wild iris. Of course, it has never sent the invitation.

I left the print shop not without, however, a few early issues of *Yugen*. In fact, I carried those copies with me several years if only to remind myself that LeRoi Jones had effectively kept me not so much from publishing in his magazine, but kept then and forever the label of "beat poet" from my name and work. And I'm still unsure whether that has been a hindrance or a godsend. Little did I know that afternoon that *Yugen* would eventually become a collector's item and those copies demand large prices, or that the poets Jones published would one day surely rime with Eliot, Ransom, Hughes and Thomas, Dylan . . . not only rime but place those poets in mothballs.

In the years to come I would from time to time catch sight of LeRoi strolling Second Avenue with his daughters, or in a bookshop, or see in the papers where he was presenting a reading of his poems. We never spoke again. I remained distressed he had not liked my poems, and perhaps . . . though I'm inclined to doubt it . . . he was distressed I had not taken copies of the magazine for sale. Little did I realize that was far from his thoughts . . . he couldn't have cared less. He had already legally changed his name as a political act, a finger to white America, and burst upon the Media scene as Amiri Baraka, playwright and poet . . . published in the haloed *Poetry* magazine, etc., and was to rock, shake and anger the world of not only American/English literature but quite possibly the foundation of government itself. His political stance would be a war cry and many warriors would rise to swell his ranks. Consequently a tremendous debt is owed LeRoi Jones. He opened tightly guarded doors for not only Blacks but poor whites as well and, of course, Native Americans, Latinos and Asian-Americans. We'd all still be waiting the invitation from the *New Yorker* without him. He taught us all how to claim it and take it back.

LeRoi and I, separately, have forded many rivers, stormed a few walls in our respective careers. He went on to become one of the few household words in American literature, shared by Allen Ginsberg and Norman Mailer. That is fine and deserving. He has worked, blood and sweat, to arrive at that position . . . a Black writer in white America, a herculian feat, a near impossibility. He accomplished this on his own strengths and genius, his oratorical and lyrical gifts and the strong will not merely to survive and his people to survive but to prevail . . . if Amiri will allow this Faulkner paraphrase.

The last ten years have found me hectically busy publishing my own poetry and coediting a magazine and press. Four years ago my partner approached me with some unpublished poems of Baraka's for the magazine. We had made an early policy that we would not publish super-star poets but reserve the pages for the young and unknown. I held back a positive response. My partner suggested I held a grudge for the rejection in *Yugen.* Nonsense, I protested. Hogwash. I was/ am an adult, can deal with the ghosts of the past. Yet, how can we be sure of hidden hurts, disappointments and the layers of grief that fold into growing skin? To make it brief, we did publish the poems as an insert supplement in *Contact/II* and simultaneously published a separate edition of bookshelf sales. In late 1983 we reissued *Reggae Or Not!* Its sales have been impressive and critical reception has been to acclaim.

The three-cornered collaboration proved successful.

That late and cold afternoon in 1957 in the Marboro bookstore on West 57th Street, I could never have guessed that one day in the deep future, the smug, arrogantly young poet/manager, myself, would ever become the copublisher of that other young, laconic and righteously angry poet, LeRoi Jones. It has been a learning process . . . if only a reminder that the world is small and that all its corners eventually meet if we stand exposed long enough for the winds to swirl down and around those corners to touch and tap the cheek.

A REMEMBRANCE: WILLARD MOTLEY

Twenty-two years later I paw the darkness of recollection, searching the dimming facts and happenstance of the first meeting with an old friend whose first book, *Knock on Any Door*, burst upon the world like the red glow of the morning star. The novel was so successful that by the time I had reached college it was presented in a comparative English literature source which boasted such luminaries as Joyce, D. H. Lawrence, Thomas Wolfe and Faulkner. The novel had been a *N.Y. Times* best seller, serialized in numerous periodicals, translated into several languages, reprinted in paperback, and filmed in Hollywood. In fact, I first read the book as a serial in the *N.Y. Daily News*.

At that time I was reading the plays of O'Neill, the poems of Poe, and the novels of W. Somerset Maugham and Erskine Caldwell . . . all authors with something of a negative perspective. I was told these writers were not healthy for me.

In Willard Motley's social study, certainly one of the best since Dickens, of a young Italian youth, product of the Denver/Chicago slums, his rebellion and demise under the forces of environment/milieu, ignorance, it was simple to relate to Motley's anti-hero. Nick Romano. The boy's motto became a universally famous battle cry: "Live fast, die young, and be a good-looking corpse." Though I was neither bred nor raised in a city slum, it was relatively easy for my young spirit and mood to embrace Nick's motto and definitely the wounded, hunted, haunted aspects of his fictionalized personality. As a teenager I was something of an outlaw myself. In my youthful, poetic outlook Nick was a fantasized self. A loner, I was trying to come to grips with life and the world around me. We shared social ostracism, parental worry, and the stigma of not only being different, but unmanageable.

During my college years in the mid '50's I struggled to grapple with the McCarthy era and the Eisenhower administration, which was to dump the country into a political and warring mess from which it would not emerge until the middle of the '70's after Viet Nam, if it has emerged at all. At this time I was still reading O'Neill and had added to my list of favorites Catullus, Flaubert, Gerard M. Hopkins, Yeats and T. S. Eliot . . . a strange group. I was dabbling with poems and fictions and leaning on brief notes from John Crowe Ransom, who attempted to place some critical direction on my poor phrasing. Werner Beyer, a professor, was prodding me away from O'Neill, Motley and company into the embrace of the romantics: Keats and Wordsworth, who fit perfectly into my rich, pastoral imagination. Werner, himself a product of Mark Van Doren and Columbia University, fed me Blake and Coleridge and admonished my vague interest in Byron and Shelley. He encouraged me to fiction rather than verse, suggested morning exercises, and forced me to complete a novella. It was, however, the poetic which inflamed my imagination, and it was this spirit which burned from the story of Nick Romano, who was to me the embodiment of the warped lyrical soul. I was so taken with Nick and *Knock on Any Door* that I chose to write a paper for the literature course, "The Poetical Element in Willard Motley's *Knock on Any Door*."

Now, I understand. Apparently I was escaping, cutting off the roots of my childhood, the painful loneness of growing up in northern New York State. The masculine/macho syndrome of the muscled, often blind, farmer empirically deaf to the softer tones of life, dead to the imagination, crusted with the utter, desperate need to survive. Of course the land, cow, tractor were more important than either Rimbaud or the Brontës. If there was leisure he might open the Bible. My own father, who escaped the rigors of farm life, was sensitive to pain yet insensitive to my own spirit and threatened my interests with his catch phrase—I had "no nose for news"— assuming I feared to walk, though I followed soon.

As a successful Black author from Chicago who never answered questions but posed problems, Willard was acutely aware of the near diabolical political effusions centering in the capitals of America, yet, in the '50's, he chose to forfeit Chicago and established residence in Cuernavaca, Mexico. There must have been a desire to broaden his scope, and even possibly act out a dream or fantasy. It is amazing he didn't choose Europe—Paris like so many authors chose after World War II. He lived some time in Cuernavaca and then moved into the *barrio* of Mexico City, and later again, bought the "pink house on the hill always stocked with beer" in Tlalpan, in the mountains over Mexico City from where he could gaze through his glass walls down into the city lights and the university campus. In the "pink house" he practically became a recluse for the last years of his life, mainly due to poor health, financial distress and the exhausting labor directed on his novel *Let Noon Be Fair.*

Willard was one of the most generous men to grace God's green earth. His first novel earned large sums of money which he used for high living and also to bail out hungry friends. There were always skeins of hangers-on dangling from his sleeves. Often he was duped by these associates. His party friends helped deplete the bank account. Willard maintained a strong belief in, and loyalty to, his brothers . . . Black, white, brown . . . and an extraordinary compassion for the degradation of the empty stomach, mind and soul. In the 1950's position and education were allowed to wealth and not necessarily to desire or need. He felt fortunate. Though *Knock on Any Door* had been written under the auspices of the Federal Writers' Project, he was born to a middle-class family who survived the '30's depression and lived, not uncomfortably, in an all white, Irish neighborhood on the south side of Chicago, the same house where the family remains. It seems now that Willard once said his grandfather had been a pullman porter, who would certainly have brought home a decent pay check, even though the job had degrading elements of servitude. Education was not denied him. During school years he was active in sports and wrote many stories on the subject. In fact, until he died in Tlalpan he never missed a ball game on the radio. He demanded all activities in the "pink house" halt until after the ninth inning. The middle-class upbringing neither shielded him nor interfered with touching life on the streets of Chicago, or, later, in Mexico City slums. As a young writer he lived on Halstead St. in Chicago, a decaying neighborhood where many Mexicans came to find homes in America. He traveled cross-country to New York by bicycle, and, still fired with the adventurous spirit, tripped to California in a broken down jalopy . . . before the Beats ever thought of setting out. He walked through a gauntlet of jobs in his young days . . . from dishwasher to farm hand. What other kinds of jobs would a Black youth with a high school education . . . which was no mean feat . . . acquire in those days! However, I would doubt that Willard would have chosen it any other way. He was quite proud of those accomplishments. He believed in pulling up by the bootstraps and independence.

It naturally fell that Willard would know empathy for the less fortunate . . . the poet who wouldn't make it, the drunk, the addict who couldn't pull out the needle, the abandoned wife, the youth deprived of inalienable rights to pursue happiness yet destroyed in the wheels of various machinations of the industrialized world. Willard spent his life as a man and artist giving. There was no bottom to the pot or purse. It was rarely refilled by anyone but himself, even though he chose the burden. The loan was almost never returned. There were few complaints, although deep in his heart he felt taken, ignored especially during those last years when the resources were petering out and his own physical strength weakened. A trace of bitterness, a sense of betrayal appears in *Let Noon Be Fair* . . . if only in the title. Yes, there were excellent reasons for the "beer til noon and the tequila across the night." He felt forgotten, knew financial trouble, knew his health was in critical danger, and was confident he would not repeat the success of *Knock on Any Door*. Quietly he closed the door to the literati. He kept a minimal number of friends and mainly Mexican neighbors, his adopted son, Sergio, and daughter-in-law, one or two houseboys to clean, garden, drive the truck for the badly needed water to run the household, and, occasionally, he admitted a visiting tourist from the States. It was impossible to sever all ties. He fed on stories of his friends and acquaintances, and offered his shoulder or purse in turn. Willard assiduously ascribed to a liberal dictum. He believed in Man and he believed in sharing, but more important he held the utmost faith in the concept of love. It would have taken the cold muzzle of a gun to his head to convince him mankind was not worthy of love and salvation. He, indeed, wrestled with problems which befell Nick Romano. But his generosity did not stop at joining the liberal club. He never marched nor waved a flag. His concern was always for the individual, the person pounded, hammered, misshapen by civilization/society. He was totally repulsed by the church and particularly the Catholic church, and considered it the cruelest despot in creation, a thief and a torturer of the poor and weak.

Willard was neither saint nor martyr. He had faults, he suffered under his own personal problems. He was not always wise in his choice of "buddies," could not control his compulsive spending, and weakened to every cry of misery. His optimism was often groundless. Friends never called wolf too often. His success and joy never blinded him to man's inhumanity to man, and devious traits. Eventually he learned not to completely trust. He never released his abiding love for the less fortunate. At times his naïvete, his gullibility, appeared almost concocted. It was easy to lose patience with his unshakable belief that the flaw in Man was not Creator given but derived from an inexplicable accident. He was not Presbyterian and could not possibly conceive of predestination. Perhaps he was not wrong. Whatever, he was adamant. It was also easy to lose patience with his digressions, his procrastinations, and, in the last years, with his tequila, especially when he demanded you tip cup for cup.

A normal day in the Motley house was to rise around eight, drive down the hill to Tlalpan for the mail, stop to read the American papers over beer in a local *tienda,* where he could greet old friends of the village, or students who paused at his table to rap about the ball game the day before. Then shop for fresh tortillas and chilis, a hunk of cheese or a cut of beef. Then home to the game if one was listed for the afternoon, and, if not, then a bout at the typewriter. Often during the middle of work he would rush from the study with an old manuscript, perhaps torn and muddy from many revisions, and ask to have it read, evaluated, saying that years before either his agent or publisher had rejected it. How could we rework it into a publishable state? These manuscripts were plays; and once he brought out his Mexican travel book, *Mi Casa Es Su Casa,* and on numerous occasions he appeared in the doorway gripping the unpublished novella, *Remember Me to Mama.* He was eager for criticism and assurance. Some afternoons were spent quietly in conversation. Willard enjoyed "shop talk" to a degree, and secretly relished gossip as it's supposed all novelists would. "Shop talk" was not backbiting, it was usually talk of form, content, prose rhythm, etc. "Maury, exactly what is the difference between the Chekovian and Maughamian short story? Which is the more successful in your opinion?" He thoroughly enjoyed discussing conflict, but his true pleasure was the building of character, assembling bits and pieces which eventually would form a whole. Nick Romano had been fitted together from three youths: a Portuguese boy, an Irish boy, and a Mexican boy . . . all youths Willard had known in Chicago while living on Halstead Street. More often than not these afternoons were pleasantly spent . . . especially if baseball were out of season. Evenings were filled with banter and games, Scrabble in Spanish and English because the houseboys, who did not speak English, could not play otherwise. Sometimes the day's work was read aloud, particularly if the piece was a finished product. Although Willard himself, a good cook, often pre-pared dinner, he rarely partook of the meal. He preferred to sit at the long dining table, discuss the possibilities, in playful manner, for a character in a proposed work, or comment on various authors he enjoyed reading: Gide, James Purdy, etc. At the end of the meal he'd place his dinner plate on the high mantle of the living room fireplace saying he would eat later, which he never did. Then he would bring out the tequila bottle, particularly if male friends arrived with guitars from Mexico City, or students came from the village with their weepy love poems to their senoritas or mothers. This would go on until near dawn. He would not allow a guest to leave or anyone of the household to retire, and if you were to lay your head on a pillow, Willard sometimes would creep into the bedroom and demand you return to the conversation or listen to his talk at the bedside. At four A.M. this could be annoying. He simply could not either say goodnight or goodbye. "Maury, wait til tomorrow." One time a planned trip to Acapulco took nearly three weeks to start. Willard was to stay and work at home. He thought of every excuse why we should wait until the next day to leave. Floods, hurricanes, disasters of all descrip-tions would be our fate should we leave on the moment. He had been severely bitten by the Mexican *mañana* bug.

Time and routine were broken by trips down to the City for "sweet sixteen parties" of friends' daughters who had come of age, occasional trips to Cuernavaca for fun and shopping and cold beer at a street cafe, or trips to the nearby river for housewater. To the best of my recall, he never sought a party, a museum, a play or a concert in the last years, yet he sur-rounded himself with newspapers, books, art, artifacts and music. He was tired, and took his entertainments at home. He turned the invitations down.

I returned to the "pink house" in Tlalpan in 1964. His finances and health were at a dangerous level. He worked less on *Let Noon Be Fair*, catnapped more, found extra time to play with his two boxers and guide his houseboy to study English. Fewer people came to his house for entertainment or solace. He ate less and drank more. Routine shifted only slightly as shadows shift. In August I moved down the hill into Mexico City proper. I wanted the flavor of living in that cosmopolitan center, to stretch, and to try my newly acquired Spanish. One month later I returned to New York.

The winter of 1964 I went to live in St. Thomas, Virgin Islands. On March 4, 1965, I bought a copy of the *New York Times* and was confronted with Willard's photograph on the obituary page. He had died in the "pink house" of gangrene of the intestine, I learned later. A friend and champion had passed away at the age of 56, his books and fame to be near obliterated within the fervor of the political movements of the 1960's. Willard Motley was branded an "Uncle Tom" and forgotten as such, unprotested.

Now there's a dimming memory which will eventually forget the warmth and humor of the man, the prodding challenge to lock the bedroom door and work, work at a project he himself had suggested the night before; a dimming memory of the excitement meeting this truly good man, the famous author who shared a dark sleeping-room house in the West Village over cups of tea and jam jars of cheap wine.

Willard never forgave me the tea, and never tired of chiding me. In huge bursts of laughter, as was his wont, he mocked the young romantic poet for offering the veteran, of all liquids, tea.

There isn't much left but a last and final letter, dated January 30, 1965, in which he wrote thanks for having remembered to send a copy of the novel, *Blood and Sand*, he'd been wanting to read; and an inquiry of the health of a mutual friend in New York who was dying of cancer, and a postscript: "The new book goes well and should be finished in less than a month now. Hope your writing is going well. As ever, Will."

How degenerate we are to suppose, presume, we can sum
up a man and his friendship of six years in a handful of pages.
Surely this is a sign of the rushed, decaying times in which we
live.

IN NAME ONLY . . . : A REVIEW

As the editor's introduction to this huge tome [*The Best of
Crazyhorse: Thirty Years of Poetry and Fiction*, edited by David
Jauss (Fayetteville: University of Arkansas Press, 1990), 468
pages] states, Crazy Horse was, indeed, an Oglala Dakota
man of tremendous stature with his people. He was known as
the "pale one" or the Light Haired Boy, and alternately, the
Glorious Warrior, "the man of the people," Curley, and the
Strange One. Born on the Plains between 1838 and 1842, he
was assassinated by a white man—a soldier—as he stepped
from a jail cell September 7, 1877 . . . Mourned by his people,
he was respected greatly by Native Americans and Anglos
alike. He truly was an epic hero. A man of great physicality,
strength, moral conviction and human integrity, a man of
silence and also of action, a dreamer and visionary. It does
seem fitting that an American literary review, *Crazyhorse,* be
named after him in honor and recognition of his greatness.
And surely editor Jauss suggests that honor in the introduction.

However, of the some 83 poems and pieces of fiction included in this 30-year retrospective not one is authored by a
Native American writer. This pays no honor to Crazy Horse
nor to his achievements as a leader. Perhaps no Native writers
have appeared in the magazine pages over these 30 years—
but it seems odd, crazy, that no Native author was worthy
enough to include . . . This is 1991 not 1877. Yet the "massacres" and "assassinations" seem to prevail.

The above fact is sad, indeed, difficult to deal with when
one looks at the incredible list of American authors collected
in this book, authors of huge reputations, some of whom may

live out this century because of the sterling gifts they possess. Obviously it was a difficult task for Jauss . . . to make choices whom to include. Surely during all this time there must have been one Native poet or storyteller of a quality to merit inclusion. A reader cannot help but wonder what Thomas McGrath, the first editor of the magazine, would think were he living at this moment and scanning down the contents.

Yet the work included in this retrospect is amazing, challenging, sparkling, with such authors as Jack Anderson, John Ashbery, Robert Bly, Carolyn Forche, Garrett Lau Hongo, Gary Soto, Charles Simic, John Updike and James Wright, though there does seem a predominance of males.

They tell us it is a free country; an editor has rights, needs and certain prejudices and biases. This bias, however, is shocking and takes away from the glory and beauty and strength of *The Best of Crazyhorse*. It is true that the great Oglala leader/warrior was buried in a sacred place—a secret place. Perhaps the contemporary Native authors have been interred beside him in the dark cave.

Readers of American literature might be encouraged to buy and read this collection. It shimmers even though there is a smudge on the sheen.

"I DO NOT WASTE WHAT IS WILD . . . ": LOUIS (LITTLE COON) OLIVER

Unless it's an American presidential inauguration, the *New York Times* rarely is known to publish an original poem. Years ago it was an excellent market for a quick buck. The Op Ed page ran poems continuously, poems by such poets as Frances Frost and Louis Ginsberg; often topical, sometimes lyrical, mostly brief. An extra joy to combat the depressing news of the day. Those poems and poets are missed by the *Times* readers.

On June 21, 1991, the *Times* published five poets celebrating the advent of summer, on its first day. Poets published were Lucie Brock-Broido, Edward Hirsch, Mona Van Duyn, Charles

Simic . . . both Pulitzer awardees . . . and a poem by Creek Indian poet Joy Harjo titled "Fishing." Her prose-poem deals with the death of a Creek elder who was a poet and storyteller, Louis (Little Coon) Oliver, born and raised in Oklahoma, Indian Territory. Oliver, born in 1904, passed away in the spring of 1991.

Ms. Harjo is an extraordinary poet of lyric and passionate power, and she brings that power of song and sense of loss into her gentle but forthright lyrical tribute to Little Coon and his fascinating and compelling humorous storytelling and serious poetry . . . At times his stories border on the erotic yet are always traditional, always wise with a wink of the eye. It is a pity Ms. Harjo's poem can not be reprinted here; this journal may well be put out of business with lawsuits from the original publisher.

Louis lived his many years in Oklahoma and came late to publication and to any type of recognition, even by his Native American literary peers. If memory is correct, it may well have been Joseph and Carol Bruchac of the *Greenfield Review* who first brought the poet into print. To the best of recall the *Times* never printed a review of any of his books in the book supplement . . . to its shame . . . It took his death to find his name in the newspaper's pages, and it took a well known, fairly established poet to memorialize him there in print. A despondent comment on contemporary culture. Corporations have denied the wider reading audience to this delightfully gifted man's truly special creativity.

We do, however, have Joy Harjo to thank for reminding society in which we all live and work, pleasure and labor, of this gentle being who passed through our light ever so quietly. We should join Ms. Harjo in her *adowe*, her thanks, for Louis Oliver's chuckle, his wisdom, his marvels of storytelling—his moving poems. We need also to thank Ms. Harjo for reminding us once again of the many fine American poets who never receive awards nor make the *New York Times* bestseller list. May the sun shine on her lyric, her song which may be the "first song" forever, and the beauty and creativity of Louis Oliver. May we all meet at the "fishing hole" in the spirit world, as Ms. Harjo suggests. Little Coon will be waiting to greet us at that Oklahoma fishing hole "under the relentless sun of the Illinois river." *Adowe.*

INTRODUCING THE POET TO THE MAN: T.S. ELIOT

How well I remember sitting in the Butler University student cafeteria surrounded by English majors . . . a few who systematically took Dylan Thomas apart, worshipping the hem of Pound and Stevens, deploring Edna St. Vincent Millay and Elinor Wiley . . . as they breathlessly awaited the newest publication of Thomas Stearns Eliot. The year was '54 and the book (or play, rather) was *The Confidential Clerk.* Eliot's *Complete Poems and Plays* had been published two years earlier and his collected criticism was to appear three years later. Little did we ever guess that as soon as he was stone cold dead in the grave his work would nearly cease to be read, and that his reputation would decline so drastically it would take a smash hit on Broadway, a musical version of his playful poems on cats, to revitalize that sadly damaged reverence. Eliot's hit play, *The Cocktail Party*—arriving on Broadway at the height of the therapy fad of the middle-class—took America figuratively by storm, made Alec Guinness a superstar and T. S. Eliot a household name equalled in poetic circles only by Allen Ginsberg and LeRoi Jones (Amiri Baraka) fifteen years later. Eliot was adored by the eggheads . . . a long forgotten epithet . . . the intellectuals, or what we considered the smart-asses. Whitman and Sandburg alike were shunned, Thomas respected by a bohemian element and not much praised by the department chair; Robinson Jeffers was cancelled out of the textbooks to which Louise Bogan had never been admitted—poets on the fringe of suspicion. Academia reigned with an iron fist; the English Department was boss, and the professor who continued to teach the "insipid" Keats or, worse, the ol' doc himself, William Carlos Williams, well, his or her job was in dire jeopardy.

It must be admitted, and though I could not or would not then intellectualize my admiration, there was fervent admiration walking the campus with trousers rolled, eating peaches, wanting to be etherized on a table and kicking rats in the street. The poetic pose, the phony spirit attached to the point that not even a curse crossed the lips. Hands folded as if in prayer, we sat and listened to the utterings, frankly, of an Eliot bore, a fellow student who sermonized on his greatness, explicating each and every syllable and punctuation in Eliot's poems. Fascinating for a green student fresh from "eggs and cheese" country. Though one secretly admired, even more than Eliot, Jeffers and Bogan, the adulation was proffered, and blessings were showered by our leader, the Eliot scholar-student.

But to this very moment the beauty and power of "The Love Song," "Gerontion," "The Waste Land" and "Sweeny Agonistes," or the play *Murder in the Cathedral,* haunt the revery, and many memorized lines come trippingly off the tongue. Much of T. S. Eliot's work is still sound and good, pleasurable to read and a joy to cat-and-mouse with.

What was lacking back at the cafeteria table amongst "toast and tea" — coffee if you were really provincial— were the facts, the bare facts of his life. Some gossip crept through, but not sufficient to grasp a real look at the human being. We knew his fabulous education at Harvard, the denial of his American citizenship, that he was an English royalist and had joined the High Church of England, had been both a publisher and banker, and was a close friend of Ezra Pound, among other wordly famous thinkers and writers. That was all common knowledge. We knew he was not only a major poet and playwright but a major literary critic whose dogma would command respect for centuries; that the color of his tie had changed English literature as Keats' height had a century before. But we knew nothing of the real man, as Eliot himself insisted upon excommunicating the man from the poet. The biography would not be important for an understanding of the poem. Hence the rejection of Dylan Thomas, who had sprawled his squalid life across the barroom floors of the English-speaking world. What Eliot did in the bathroom, in the bedroom or in the rose garden was simply none of our business; what he ate for breakfast was known only by his cook; what he revealed to his preacher-confessor was locked up in the confessional box not to be sold to the tabloids. He was not to be Yeats' "public man." Since his death on January 4, 1965, that gossip has slowly leaked out: his first wife's incarceration in an insane asylum, his alleged though not proven homosexuality, etc. . . . The dirt of his life escaped and is now equated and analyzed with his art.

Peter Ackroyd's fine new biography of Eliot [*T. S. Eliot: A Life*, 1984] not only examines this life minutely in the raw, and explores the creative efforts with intelligence and acuteness, but helps to replenish esteem for his work and to place Eliot's genius in proper light and justified respect. The language is slow and often wordy (but Eliot himself was wordy). Ackroyd's style certainly does not reflect the current mode of essayists such as Tom Wolfe or Susan Sontag. There remains a pleasure in the style, a little old-fashioned, and the respect for the language Eliot so desperately hones and jewelled. *A Life* is a good read, fascinating and intelligent, succinct as those peaches we ate walking the Butler campus. A better biography can't be imagined of this twentieth-century giant.

PROLIFERATION: ISAAC JOGUES

My friend Rochelle Ratner invited me to spend a few days at her new country home outside Granville, N.Y. She asked me north as much for my "expertise" in flora and fauna as for my cooking, she joked. She had developed a need to know daylilies from hawkweed, raspberries from poison ivy, fishers from house cats. Rochelle had been born and reared in Atlantic City and had spent ten years living in Soho, N.Y.C., an area not inhabited too frequently by fishers and goldenrod. She was then in the country and wanting "to learn my land."

The first day north was spent acquainting myself with the lay of the acreage, and acquainting Rochelle with the beauties of her four square: her loganberry brambles on the knoll, the poison ivy she was allergic to, the chokecherry, the wild geraniums, the fruit growing on the pear. The next day we spent driving.

Rochelle was familiar with my abiding interests in Hendricks (Aroniakteka), the Mohawk chief, and Sir William Johnson, an important early settler in central New York State, and one of the leading British officers at the time of the French and Indian War, 1755. I was working on a new collection of poems dealing with their lives and the war, especially the life and times of Molly Brant (Tekonwatonti), the elder sister of the infamous Joseph Brant (Thayendanegea). Molly had been Johnson's common-law wife though he'd had numerous off-spring by a motley assortment of concubines. Lake George was a mere twelve miles, and we set our sights to locate the battlefield where Hendricks lost his life, but where Johnson, however, scored a smashing victory, made himself legendary and changed the course of American history forever.

Lake George, like Lake Placid higher up the Adirondacks, is an American disaster. It's sardined with curio shops, McDonalds and teeny-boppers clad in swimsuits. The environment is crowded and confused with phony antique shops, plastic pizzerias and expensive amusement parks, all to the delight of tourists escaping the rigors of summering in New York City.

We found the battlefield and a single battlement standing with a near-nude couple sunning on the furthest rampart. The park's warden gave us a brochure, which indicated a monument to both Hendricks and Johnson, also an unknown soldier's monument, the ruin itself, and something described as being an "Indian Monument." That struck our fancy. Reading further, to my horror, it announced the Indian Monument was in reality a commemoration of the discovery of Lake

264   Essays and Reviews

George, in 1646, by none other than Isaac Jogues, the Jesuit missionary. We didn't know whether to laugh or sling stones. In April of 1982 North Country Community College Press released my new collection of poems, *Blackrobe: Isaac Jogues.* Naturally, my appetite was whetted. I won't go into a heated quibble of this fraudulent example of American history except to say that the Jesuit Father Isaac was put to death by the Mohawks for having tampered with the people's religion, among other reasons, on October 18, 1646, which was certainly a little late in the north calendar year to be discovering lakes which Iroquois, Algonquins, Hurons, and Abenakis had plied their boats across for centuries. He may have been the first European to view Lake George, but I have some doubt even of that.

But there was Jogues brassed larger than life on a high pedastal looking north over the lake with his blessed communion fingers extended behind a closed and locked iron fence. A cement path led to the monument and we insisted upon taking the regulated walk. We were met by a staggering, shocking surprise. Within the iron grill the ground floor was swept with wild strawberry vines whose leaves had already turned red under the hot sun. The leaves bore no fruit. The strawberry is the first natural fruit of the eastern spring. It is the symbol of life to the Iroquois people. It is the name of my press from which I publish, exclusively, Native American poets and artists. Hence the shock. Venus's-looking-glass blossomed amongst the vines. A careless tourist had tossed a pair of scarlet socks before the momument. I almost wrote altar. The shrine was half encircled behind by both cedar and white pine, which are very important to Iroquois people. It was under the great white pine that Deganawidah planted the war weapons of the Five Nations (Mohawk, Onondaga, Seneca, Cayuga and Oneida) once he had convinced these Nations to join into a peaceful League. Cedar is sometimes used in medicine, and sometimes in smoke. It holds special properties. I tucked a pinecone in my pocket, and remembered a letter received sometime back from Bro. Benet

Tvedten, a Benedictine monk, who had visited the Jogues shrine at Auriesville, N.Y., and pronounced the shrine an abysmal carnival. (Bro. Benet, a fine man and good friend, wrote an afterward to *Blackrobe.*)

On inspecting the monument at close range, we discovered two friezes on either side of the stone. The left frieze was of René Goupil, also a Jesuit martyr, though never sainted by the church. On the opposite, outside wall was a carving of Jean de La Lande, a novice who had accompanied Jogues on his last journey into the Mohawk villages, who was put to death immediately after Jogues had been dispatched. Behind young Jean an unidentified Mohawk warrior had been carved into the frieze.

Out of the corner of my eye I spotted a small hornet's nest in the pit of Jogues' right arm, raised obviously in blessing. His communal fingers had been chopped off. Another nest was attached to the brass behind his moccasined foot, raised in step. We wondered about these significant natural symbols: he is still not welcome to the land.

I plucked a strawberry leaf to carry home and press within the pages of my book, *Blackrobe.*

Jogues had been successful planting the seeds not only of his Catholicism, but also of destruction which took root and was nourished by his blood, and which still to this moment grows in hearts and pocketbooks of Americans who sell their shorelines, crack open their mountains, cover their desert with cement, blacken the beautiful skies with pollution, murder their fellow creatures with bullets.

Later in the afternoon while tramping through the high grasses and within the low sumac of Rochelle's four acres, I waded through vetch and black-eyed susans to discover my friend's strawberry patch. We were delighted. Fruit hung on the vines no larger than the size of a thumbnail. They were sweetly delicious. They had not only survived but proliferated.